CAF **HOW TO** GU

Producin
Promotional
Materials

A step by step guide for small voluntary organisations

KAREN GILCHRIST

© 1998 Karen Gilchrist

Published by Charities Aid Foundation
Kings Hill
West Malling
Kent ME19 4TA

Series Editor   Graham Watson
Editor   Myra Bennett

Design and production   Eugenie Dodd Typographics

Printed and bound in Great Britain by Bell & Bain Limited, Glasgow

A catalogue record for this book is available from the British Library.

ISBN 1–85934–084–9

Telephone   +44 (0) 1732 520000
Fax   +44 (0) 1732 520001
E-mail   Cafpubs@caf.charitynet.org
Web site   http://www.charitynet.org

Contents
....

About the author

Karen Gilchrist is a researcher and writer. She is director of the media and communications company Resource Base which works in social, educational and cultural affairs. Karen was a journalist with the magazines *Marketing Week* and *Televisual* before working in television as a social action researcher. She has been a cross-media co-ordinator with the charity Community Service Volunteers and worked for TVS Education and Community before helping to set up Resource Base. The company runs media and communications training courses for charities and produces a wide range of resources in all media.

Introduction
· · · · · · · · ·

Every day we are bombarded with images, marketing messages, subtle branding and in-your-face advertising. Companies, individuals, governments and charities are all jostling to attract people's attention with their promotional materials.

In this image-conscious age we need to consider how we present our organisation – whether it be on paper, on video, on computer screen or in any other medium. Of course, any information presented in these forms needs to fit in with the wider approach of the organisation. Everything from how people answer the phone through to how people are welcomed face-to-face is part of your corporate identity.

In this book we are going to focus on published materials, exploring some of the ways you can present and promote your charity effectively. We look at some of the general principles and different approaches.

You might be able to afford to commission outside agencies to do some of the work. Alternatively you might have skilled staff or volunteers to draw on. Both of these eventualities are covered.

- We begin with an overview. This first chapter deals with the need to have an identified person in charge of image and promotional materials. We look at the need for style guidelines and consistency of approach. Some general points are then made about the kind of image you might want and the messages you would like to give out.

- The overview goes on to consider where you are and how much scope you and your organisation have for change. Finally, we talk about flexibility and the difference between very prescriptive rules and broader guidelines.

- The next chapter is all about logos. We look at their importance and the ways you can develop brands and sub-brands. The section covers the different elements that might make up a logo; how you can gradually develop a logo rather than starting afresh; and some of the practical issues to consider.

- Chapter 3 is a large portion of the book. It covers many different types of printed materials. These include: letterheads; faxes; leaflets; brochures; annual reviews; newsletters; visual aids; posters; adverts; fliers; postcards and greetings cards; exhibition panels; certificates; and internal documents. There are suggestions about both format and content. We also discuss accessibility.

- The next chapter looks at working with designers and printers. You might work with people within your organisation, but you will probably deal at some point with external agencies. There are some useful checklists for getting quotes; developing ideas and briefs; proofing and signing things off; and delivery, storage and distribution.

- Chapter 5 covers audio cassettes. We look at the two main kinds of audio: first talking books, where someone simply reads a leaflet or book onto tape; then tailor-made cassettes which are newly scripted productions.

- Video is the focus of the next section. We consider some of the different uses you might have for a video and different approaches to getting it made. There are tips on effective commissioning; the use of spokespeople; ensuring branding is seen; and packaging considerations.

- Chapter 7 looks at the opportunities provided by the Internet. We talk about gradually developing a presence on the Web. Then we look at the practicalities of developing and maintaining a Website.

- Next we turn to CD-ROM and discuss some of the ways this medium can be used to promote your organisation.
- Merchandise is often developed on an ad hoc basis. We suggest the need for guidelines to be applied in each case. Chapter 9 looks at different types of merchandise, how to develop guidelines and how to check that they are applied.

Finally, we signpost additional sources of help and information.

CHAPTER ONE

Overview

Many organisations identify an individual to develop and look after their image and house style. They give this person and their team the authority to work on new initiatives and to give guidance to other people in the organisation.

Who takes responsibility?

If you don't make it clear that someone is in ultimate charge of design and promotional matters then you could easily find that your organisation is using a range of different letterheads and posters in a variety of styles, contributing to a general dilution of your brand.

CASE STUDY

One Hampshire-based charity discovered that not only was one of its departments using a completely new design of letterhead, but it was also breaking the law by using paper with no details of its charity number and registered address.

The person who is given responsibility for house style and marketing issues will want to have a degree of creative freedom. They will, of course, be answerable to their line manager or an appropriate committee. But it is extremely difficult to design by committee. A committee can set a context, give guidance about what is considered appropriate and can make a selection from a set of options. But a committee rarely comes up with inspirational, innovative and experimental ideas. Instead a committee can give someone a brief and sanction their work.

So, who within your organisation might take charge of developing your image and house style? It should be someone responsible for PR and marketing. As with all such roles larger charities will have a whole department supporting the work on this area, smaller ones will have one member of staff or one volunteer juggling this with many other activities. It is important to consult widely within your organisation. You might find it helpful to contact The Media Trust if you want the advice of media professionals on a voluntary basis.

The need for consistency

What are the dangers you might face if you don't have a house style and simple set of guidelines? You can miss many opportunities to reinforce the main messages you want to get across – to workers, supporters and clients. If you don't have guidelines, you might give out inappropriate and inaccurate messages.

Think of some of the big brands. They use every opportunity to reinforce their identity. They might make strong use of their colour – examples include Orange, Cadbury's *Yellow Pages*, and *The Financial Times*. They might give a high profile to a symbol – such as the BT piper. Catchlines are also repeated until they are drummed into us – such as Asda's 'pocket the difference'.

And it is repetition that is the key. If you keep on saying the same thing, giving out the same message, people begin to recognise you and to associate you with particular causes, achievements and activities. If everyone in your organisation is saying something different, then people will either be confused or just unaware of your work.

Your image and message

. . . .

So, what are you trying to say through the logo you use, the fonts you select, the kinds of paper you print on: what is your organisation's look and feel?

Many charities want their literature and other materials to say that they:

- are responsible and committed;
- remain rooted in the community;
- make a difference;
- could do more if they had more funding;
- are professional and work to high standards;
- are not overfunded or wasteful;
- are modern and forward looking;
- are open and accessible to all.

It might be worth developing a similar list for your own organisation. Then, take a look at your materials to see whether or not they achieve some or all of this.

Your starting point and the scope for change

. . . .

Different charities will be at different stages of development. Their images, logos, branding and materials reflect this. It is important not to rush into change for change's sake, but first to analyse where your organisation is, what you have achieved so far and how radical you want to be.

The following questionnaire is designed to help you identify where your organisation is in terms of design and promotional development. There are no right or wrong answers, and no analysis at the end. You should simply run through the questions to get a feel for your current position: the amount of change that has already taken place, and your freedom to introduce new ideas.

1 How long has your charity been in existence?

2 Has it always had the same logo? If no, how many times has the logo changed? What were the reasons for the changes? How radical were they?

3 How long have you been using the current letterhead?

4 How many times has the letterhead design been changed?

5 How many different versions of letterhead are currently being used?

6 Is there any central co-ordination of letterhead design?

7 How many people in your organisation produce leaflets, newsletters, reports and other literature?

8 Is there any central co-ordination for design and print production?

9 Do you work with outside agencies? If yes, how many different agencies do you work with? How do you select them? Do you issue them with any style guidelines? Who is responsible for working with them?

10 How do you produce the editorial content for leaflets, adverts and other materials? Is there an internal checking process?

11 How do you produce merchandise, such as badges, T-shirts, cups etc.? Are there any guidelines in existence? Do you have preferred suppliers?

12 Do you have a stock control system? Do you know when supplies of literature and materials will run low?

13 How do you budget for the production of materials? Do you invite comparable quotes from different suppliers?

14 Are you part of an umbrella organisation? Are there guidelines you need to follow?

Rules versus guidelines

Throughout this book we make a variety of suggestions about adopting certain guidelines. Some organisations will have a set of templates and rules that they follow rigorously. Others will have a broad set of guidelines which leave plenty of freedom for interpretation. How prescriptive you are will depend on your particular team and circumstances.

CASE STUDY
....

Scope has a booklet of guidelines on how to use its distinctive blue and orange logo correctly. The name and logo change (from the Spastics Society) in 1994 provided an opportunity to develop a more consistent approach at all levels of the organisation as Creative Services Manager Nigel Tuckett explains.

'Before the change of name and logo many groups and projects were doing their own thing. The new identity helped us to bring things together and create a unified approach.

'The thing to remember is that new people join the organisation all the time. The corporate identity is part of the induction pack, but training and monitoring procedures are also helpful. We run workshops for our managers so that they can become local ambassadors in how to use the identity effectively.'
....

CHAPTER TWO

Logos

You might have inherited a logo that is just there and you live with it. However, it's worth thinking about whether your logo is still working for you.

This is not to suggest that you change things for the sake of it. In many cases all that is needed is a tweak or perhaps a change of emphasis. Your logo may be working well in which case no change is needed. But it might be reassuring to work through the following section to check that your logo is as effective as it could be.

The importance of logos

What is a logo and why is it important? A logo is your organisation's badge – it can be an image, symbol, or words (or a combination of them). It should sum up the spirit and personality of your organisation. At a glance someone from outside should get a feel for your values or what you stand for.

You might want people to appreciate that you are a well-established charity with a considerable heritage. You might use historical symbolism and traditional fonts. Alternatively, you might want people to appreciate that you are a young and vibrant group. In this case you might go for bright colours, modern fonts and more abstract imagery.

Simon Heron, from design agency Three Men and a Suit says:
'A logo should be simple and so strong that it will work even if
it's produced as a potato print.'

Nigel Tuckett, of Scope, says: 'The orange flourish of Scope's logo
gives it a lift and makes it recognisable. And if you can cover up
half a logo and still know whose it is, then the logo's working.'
· · · · · · · · ·

Take a look at your logo. What does it say about who you are
and what you do? Perhaps the name of your organisation says it
all, and you want this to be used in a clear and uncluttered way.
That's fine. You don't have to go for overcomplicated or over-
subtle approaches.

However, words and images change their meaning over time.
Organisations change too. So, what was once an accurate
reflection of your work may no longer be appropriate.

Brands and sub-brands
· · · · · · · ·
Many organisations have sub-groups or departments within
them. Sometimes groups come together in a loose affiliation
or network. Sometimes a single charity will have various semi-
autonomous branches or departments. If possible, a theme
should run through them all to show some sort of connection.

An informal network shows a link through a standard message
and logo at the base of each group's materials. In this case, the
organisations retain their own corporate brands. However,
branches or departments within a single organisation might
use a single design or a variation on it. This variation would be
a sub-brand and it could be more or less subtle – the typeface
might be the same, the colours and words might change.

This particular issue is discussed in more detail in the section on
letterheads on page 23.

Images, words, typefaces and straplines
·········

We have already seen that a logo can be made up of one or more elements. It can be a word, letters (perhaps an acronym), symbol, or any combination of these. The font (typeface) might be particularly distinctive. Many organisations have a phrase or strapline, giving a little more information about what they do. If you are using a strapline then:

- use no more than 10 words;
- avoid the use of humour;
- try to capture the spirit of your work;
- use simple unambiguous words;
- use active doing-words.

If you are using an image or symbol then try to:

- go for a simple, striking and strong image;
- ensure there is no opportunity for misinterpretation – field test it and don't be offended by people's honest instant reactions;
- don't use an image for the sake of it, ask what it is adding/saying;
- consider how it could be caricatured.

Degrees of change
·········

Changing your logo doesn't necessarily mean throwing out the old one and coming up with something completely new. Perhaps your logo is beginning to feel slightly tired and old fashioned. Yet, at the same time it is widely recognised and triggers an instant positive reaction. If this is the case you might want to retain it, but introduce a new more modern font, or switch to a brighter colour. You might change your strapline. You might simplify any images you are working with.

At the beginning of 1998 the disability care charity, The Leonard Cheshire Foundation, renamed itself Leonard Cheshire and adopted a distinctive new logo. This followed a year-long period of consultation with service users, staff and volunteers.

The word Foundation was dropped to prevent people from thinking that it was a grant-making trust. The logo was also modernised to reflect a modern and forward-thinking charity.

The old logo featured a red feather surrounded by a circular frame with the words The Leonard Cheshire Foundation. The new logo consists of three elements – the name Leonard Cheshire, the red feather and the strapline 'creating opportunities with disabled people'.

Marketing Manager Dave Dunn says: 'The changes appear modest but were very important in creating a stronger visual identity at both national and local levels. The logo allows every service to retain its individual and regional identity but simultaneously demonstrate that it is part of a wider organisation.'
·········

Practical considerations
············

When you are making changes to your logo and associated materials there are some practical considerations to bear in mind.

First, you need to have an agreed budget and acceptable quotes from designers before proceeding. And it's worth ensuring that designers inform you of any additions to these estimates as they arise. Ways of working with designers and other external agencies are discussed in Chapter 4. Your designers will be aware of the following points, but it's worth bearing them in mind and ensuring that anyone on an approval committee considers them too.

- Think about the different ways in which your logo will be used – in print, on the Web, on merchandise, on faxes, etc.

How easy will it be to reproduce in different media? How clear will it appear?

- Adding colours will add costs to all of your printing. If you go for very striking colours these might not be easy to produce when you use four-colour printing. Instead you might always have to add spot colour for your logo. And if you go for silver and gold this costs even more!

- You need to see how the logo works both in colour and in black and white. A logo in striking colours isn't just potentially expensive, it might also look strange in black and white. Will it work if it's reversed, that is when it appears as a white logo on a black background?

When you are satisfied with your logo ask your designer to produce various versions as artwork. Other designers or printers can then reproduce the logo accurately.

A commentary on what can be done and what can't be done with it is also helpful. You can then issue this to other parts of the organisation and to relevant partners if you are working on joint projects.

Such a commentary might say:

- if used in a colour publication, the logo should always appear in two colours (pantone numbers xx and yy);

- if used in black and white the words and image should all appear in black;

- if used in another colour the words and images should all appear in that single colour;

- the image and words can be used as white reversed out of black or another single colour.

A commentary can be worked up into a more detailed style guide. You can also make the logo and templates available on disc or CD. A style guide might include:

- information on how to use the logo in all stationery, including detailed positioning guidelines;

- samples of stationery with the logo;

- information on how to use the logo on all other printed materials;
- samples of those materials;
- samples of what is not permitted.

Using logos on vehicles

You might have one or more minibuses providing transport to staff, volunteers and clients. These provide a mobile advertising opportunity. You can give details of your organisation and what services you provide. You can also include relevant sponsor logos. The minibus will promote your work to potential clients and funders. It gives you an opportunity to raise your profile as you go about your daily work.

If you do decide to go for a big splash on the side of a minibus then it is vital you keep it in good condition. If you drive around in a dirty or rusty vehicle with your logo emblazoned on it, then people will get the impression that your charity is on the verge of collapse.

If you don't have a minibus you might have a car owned or leased by the organisation. This can also be branded appropriately to take your message out on location.

CASE STUDY

A number of Councils of Voluntary Service run community transport schemes. Their logos and details of their service are featured on the side and back of the minibuses. This helps other roadusers to be aware of their work. It also helps potential users to see the service in operation.

If your charity doesn't own any vehicles, you can always use in-car or bumper stickers to promote your work.

Car dealers, design agencies and sign writers can all provide advice on what might be appropriate for your vehicle. They are listed in *Yellow Pages*.

Using logos on signs, banners and flags

·········

Your offices, shopfronts or buildings can promote a message to the outside world. You might want to have a sign which displays your logo clearly and briefly summarises your work. Check with your local authority planning department to see what kind of signage you are allowed to erect.

CASE STUDY
·········
Age Concern shops are clearly branded. The logo is used effectively to reinforce the rest of the charity's branding. And the shops make the most of the advertising space on the front of their buildings.
·········

Within your buildings you can also provide branded signage. This will help to reinforce your identity. Use the appropriate typefaces and colours. You probably won't need to include your logo on every sign. Design agencies and sign writers can produce these for you. You can mix off-the-shelf signs with specially produced ones. The cost will reflect the amount of design and production necessary.

You might also want to have a flag or banner outside one of your buildings to promote your work. Once again it is essential to check first with your local authority planning department to find out what is permitted. Flags and banners mean that your organisation can be seen from a greater distance. People suddenly become aware that within those four walls some essential work is going on. Audio visual companies, merchandise companies and design agencies can all co-ordinate the production of flags and banners.

CHAPTER THREE

Developing printed materials

In this chapter we look at a range of different printed materials – from letterheads and fax sheets through to newsletters and internal documents. If you are revamping your logo and creating style guides then you will probably address many of the issues covered below. But, even if you are happy with your logo and the general standard of your printed materials you might want to look at a specific item – like a newsletter. If this is the case, you should consult the relevant section.

Letterheads

It is vital to have a clear and appropriate letterhead. Each day you will probably work your way through many sheets of your letterhead. And there's always someone on the receiving end, forming an opinion about your organisation.

Surprisingly, though, many organisations still run out of letterhead and move on to using photocopies of the original paper. This not only creates a bad impression it is a false economy – when you go for a reasonable professional print run the individual sheets probably cost the same or less than photocopying.

If your organisation is small, it's worth considering that a desk-top-published black and white letterhead, run off through an office printer, is cheaper and of higher quality than a photocopy.

Your letterhead will be seen by potential sponsors, individual donors, clients, potential clients, workers and others. A scrappy piece of paper might make them regard you as amateur and put them off. Simple clean high quality paper might not make them support you instantly, but it will convince them that you are professional, with high standards.

Having established the need for a good-looking letterhead, let's turn now to some of the detail.

Layout considerations

Before trying to put the various bits of information onto the page, it's worth making a list of everything that needs to go on to your letterhead, some of it essential to comply with the law and some of it useful. Then prioritise.

To comply with the law you must include:

- your organisation's name;
- registered address;
- VAT number;
- charity number.

You might also include:

- logo;
- mailing address/es;
- phone number;
- fax number;
- text phone number;
- e-mail address;
- Web address;
- affiliation to a network;
- parent organisation;
- sponsor logos;
- quality standard;
- patron;
- senior executives.

Some or all of these can appear in either margin, the header or the footer of the page. They can be more or less prominent.

Most organisations opt to put their logo at the top of the page – some go for the left hand corner, some for the right and some for the centre. The rise of sponsor logos and partnership working means that associate logos tend to appear as well: these often go along the bottom. Using the top for your own organisation's logo picks it out from the others and creates a clear identity.

You can frame your logo so that it is separated from the rest of the information; you can box your logo and contact details; or you can allow it to remain free on the page.

But if you put information in either side margin, it's worth thinking about how this will affect the layout of any letters. Will writers be forced to use an unusually wide left or right hand margin? Will information in the margin get confused with the content of the letter? Even if you can make a distinction between printed letterhead and text by using colour, this could be lost if your letter is photocopied.

Putting information in side margins or in bars of colour can look smart. So don't automatically rule it out. Just test it through your office printer and let colleagues give their opinion.

Personalised/tailored letterheads

When you are developing your letterhead design you might want to think about producing various versions within an overall family. It might be that particular senior members of the team have letterheads with their names and contact details listed. Alternatively, individual departments might have slightly different information – perhaps reflected in different colour combinations and contact details.

Sponsor credits

In some cases it will be appropriate to have a major donor or sponsor's logo on your letterhead. This might be for some specific project letterhead or it might be on all of your stationery.

It's important to liaise with the relevant people within the sponsor organisation: to get the artwork for their logos and any rules on how the logo may be used. You need to make it clear from the positioning of their logo and any accompanying statement that they are a funder. You are not writing to people on your donor or sponsor's behalf, you are contacting people in your own right.

Compliment slips and business cards

These will contain less information but reflect the style used in your letterhead. With both compliment slips and business cards you have a choice between going for the more conventional landscape (wide and short) style and the less usual portrait (tall and thin).

Compliment slips tend to be fairly standard in their layout and message – with as much space as possible for a personal note from the sender and a simple 'with thanks' or 'with compliments'.

Business cards, though, offer more scope for creativity. You might want to develop an unusual business card that the recipient won't want to throw away – because it has a different texture, is an unusual size or opens out like a greeting tag. You might print on the reverse of the business card, giving details of particular projects, case studies or how people can support your charity.

Of course, going for an unusual business card design will cost more. However, as a marketing tool you might consider it to be worth the investment.

Envelopes

Off-the-shelf envelopes suit most organisations. But you might want to produce labels which enable you to re-use envelopes that are sent in to your organisation, especially if you are a small charity with limited funds. Such labels are produced by professional printers. They work with standard sizes of labels overprinted with your particular details.

On the other hand, if you are running a special project, you might want to have envelopes with your logo, address and a message on. This allows you to reinforce your branding, be quite upfront with a fundraising message, and, at the same time, enclose literature or letters on other matters. Again you need to work with a professional printer and, possibly, a design agency.

It is usually more cost effective to have envelopes, letterheads and other branded stationery produced at the same time.

Faxes

Layout considerations

There is no point in using your best headed paper for faxes which come out black and white at the other end on a quality of paper which is out of your control. Instead, it makes sense to have specially desk-top-printed fax header sheets (unless you are faxing directly from your pc). This will also ensure that you are working with a sharp black and white version of your logo rather than a coloured version that doesn't fax well.

Sometimes the very top and bottom of a fax don't come out clearly – it all depends on the receiver's fax machine. So, try to keep information away from the edges.

Important information

It is also important to make it clear who the fax is from and how to get hold of you – by fax, phone or any other method!

You might want to include some prompts such as To, From, Date, Number of pages, etc. Many organisations find it useful to have a pick list highlighting the type of document it is or the kind of response they expect, eg for your information; reply as soon as possible, etc.

One final point on faxes: check the set up on your machine. Ensure that any data your fax adds as it sends a document is accurate. This might include date and time, your fax number, and your organisation name. Do some test faxes if necessary to friendly neighbouring organisations and take a look at the results.

Sometimes fax machines need a clean – yours might be leaving an unsightly line down all the faxes you send. You may not discover this unless you periodically send test faxes.

Leaflets and factsheets

In the course of your work you will probably produce a variety of different leaflets: perhaps giving information about specific projects or issues; or highlighting roles and opportunities within your organisation.

Templates

Even if you are producing quite a simple A4 factsheet or an A5 leaflet from a folded sheet of A4, it's worth having a template to work to. This is for two main reasons:

- consistency and repetition will reinforce your branding and help people to recognise your organisation and its work;
- working to a template makes life a lot easier – you can be creative within the guidelines but you don't have to start your thinking from scratch each time.

Some of the things that you might cover in your template are:

- general rules for the layout – position of your logo; position of sponsor's logo; use of pictures; position of title;
- guidance on the appropriate fonts to use – for headings, sub-headings, text etc.;
- notes on working with different audiences and meeting the needs of these audiences (eg large print and/or Braille, picture-based material);
- standard contact details and disclaimers.

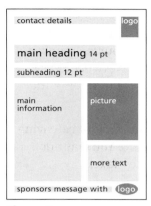

Figure 1

Format

When you are developing individual leaflets you will have to decide on the appropriate format. The main limitations are money and creative ideas.

You can work on a large tabloid scale or small pocket-book level. You can gatefold leaflets (fold them in two places so that a piece of A4 folds down to fit into a standard DL sized envelope). You can have leaflets cut to specific shapes (probably most appropriate for fundraising or event invitations).

Figure 2

Your budget, audience, the word count and time available will all play a part in the format you eventually go for. If in doubt, A4 folded down to A5 or gatefolded are two of the most straightforward approaches that should be quick and easy to produce.

Factsheets are generally printed onto A4. You might develop a standard factsheet style of paper which you overprint.

Content

When planning the content of each leaflet or factsheet you need to be very clear about why you are producing it. This will help you to come up with a simple title. It will also help staff and volunteers to know how to use it effectively in response to enquiries and in their day to day work.

One approach is to state at the beginning of the leaflet that: 'this leaflet is for anyone who wants to know more about xxx. It is one in a series of leaflets produced by xxx. You can call xxx for further information.'

The leaflet itself should be written in a simple conversational style. This will draw people in, make them feel comfortable and help them to understand your various messages. Even if your leaflet is targeted at medical staff, try to keep it simple so that it's easy to take in. Don't try to impress potential sponsors with lots of buzz-words and business-speak.

Clear headings throughout will help people to find the precise information they are looking for.

Most importantly, all leaflets should have contact details and pointers to further sources of help.

Referencing

If you are developing a series of leaflets it's worth giving them a unique reference number. This will help you to deal with orders and queries. Part of the reference should indicate the date when the leaflet was produced and the issue number. Then if leaflets

change over time, you can ensure people are using the most
up-to-date copy.

Brochures

The principles behind brochure development are similar to
those for leaflets. Brochures are more substantial and colourful;
more promotional in nature. As with leaflets it is important to
ask why you're producing a brochure and who it is for.

Your purpose and audience

The purpose of your brochure could be to:

- raise awareness of your organisation and work (amongst the
  local community; nationally; internationally; amongst
  existing supporters; amongst potential supporters; amongst
  clients, workers and volunteers; amongst the media, etc.);

- report on (and review) one or more projects (for your staff
  and volunteers; for people working in similar areas; for your
  funders and potential funders);

- disseminate good practice (to people working in similar
  areas; to your staff and volunteers);

- fundraise/highlight opportunities for support and
  involvement (for existing and potential supporters).

Being clear about the purpose of the brochure will help you to go
for the right approach. Defining your intended audience will
help you to write it appropriately and to calculate the right sort
of print run, (see page 68).

Format

Brochures tend to be produced less frequently than leaflets and
to a higher print quality. There is usually a lot more information
in them, along with more illustrations and photographs. So
they tend to be A4 and no smaller than A5, no larger than A3.

You might decide to have a glossy cover using four colours and
photographs. Inside, you might go for one or two colours. The

one colour might be black, but you can go for any dark colour, eg blue, green or purple – the text is usually still easy to read.

If you are using two colours then you can include 'duotone' photographs which combine two colours. These give the photos a lift and give a different feel to straightforward black and white photography. The use of duotone photographs can help to make a publication feel more modern and lively.

The cover might be sealed for protection or laminated to give it a sheen and different feel.

Content

Because brochures usually contain more information than leaflets it's worth providing a summary at the beginning, and a contents page to help people find their way through. It is easier to read a brochure if the information is delivered in small chunks, broken up with clear headings, lots of obvious sub-headings and relevant pictures.

Many smaller charities work with freelance writers – either to write the entire brochure, or to edit some copy that they have prepared. This allows for professional input at a reasonable cost. There are various ways to find a freelance writer or copy editor. *The NUJ Freelance Directory* is a good source of information and contains regional listings of freelances with details of people's special interests. For further information contact the NUJ on 0171- 278 7916. *Yellow Pages* and other directories can also be useful. Some freelances advertise in charity magazines. Word of mouth recommendations are very helpful.

Education packs/materials

There are a number of reasons why you might decide to produce an education pack as part of your promotional work.

You might want to have a handy document to send to students when they ring up wanting to know more. Or you might want to raise awareness amongst primary or secondary school children by producing some classroom-based materials. Not only will the students learn about your organisation and the issues you are concerned with, they could also pass on some of the information to their families and friends.

In this section we are looking at the sort of pack which is designed for teachers to use in the classroom. The student information pack can be made up of the brochures and leaflets described above.

Establishing a need and curriculum relevance

Many organisations produce or sponsor education packs. Some charge quite large sums of money for their materials. Others supply packs at little or no cost to schools.

Before producing any educational pack though, it's essential to carry out some research into similar packs and what teachers actually want or need.

If you are developing a pack to be used across the UK, you need to consider the different curriculum guidelines and targets issued in England and Wales, Scotland and Northern Ireland. Education is an ever-changing area, with new ideas, technology and techniques being introduced. These might affect your plans and you have to be ready to adapt accordingly.

Format

You might want to make use of technology – putting materials on the Web, making a CD-ROM or video. Often a video is stimulating, leading to discussion points rather than specific learning. CD-ROM and Websites usually develop print a stage further. We look at all these media on pages 79–107. Here the focus is on the printed element.

Education packs usually contain:

- Notes for teachers – explaining how the pack might be used, giving background information and suggesting further sources of information.

- Lesson or activity ideas – either directed at the teacher or as prepared photocopiable handouts.
- INSET section – this provides teacher training materials, enabling teachers to build up their own skills and knowledge base before tackling an area.

Sometimes it is appropriate to put individual sheets into a folder. At other times a booklet is the right format. You might also want to include a wallchart to act as a reminder after the lessons have been delivered (most appropriate if you are targeting primary schoolchildren).

A folder is useful if you are producing a pack which covers many different curriculum areas. It enables different teachers to pick out lesson plans and ideas for their specific subject area. Folders are also helpful if teachers are expected to gather further relevant materials such as magazine and newspaper cuttings, local leaflets, etc. Booklets can be appropriate for primary schools – where a single teacher often teaches more than one subject, or for single subjects at secondary schools.

Remember that your resource will probably go onto a shelf alongside many other resources. So pay particular attention to the appearance of the spine of your pack.

Content

The actual content of your pack will reflect your interests and the relevant curriculum area. If you are covering environmental issues then you might want to refer to some guidelines produced by the Centre for Environmental Education. The CEE has developed advice on some of the issues that should be tackled by environmental education resources.

Schools are working towards quite rigorous targets and with packed timetables. If your resource is to be well-used it has to help teachers deliver some of their set curriculum areas. So, you might find it helpful to work closely with a teacher or inspector/advisor as you develop your ideas.

At all times you need to use language that is appropriate but not patronising. Different perspectives should be presented so that the pack doesn't become propaganda.

Activity ideas are very useful to teachers. You might suggest interesting ways of encouraging debate, exploration, creativity, experimentation and the delivery of information. When you are suggesting activities you should also provide details of:

- how long the activity is expected to take;
- any preparation work required;
- additional materials needed;
- learning objectives;
- an overall quick summary;
- extension activities (ways of developing the activity further).

There are a number of educational resource production companies – they develop resources using print or combining print with video. Their details are included in the *IVCA Handbook*. The education department at your local council might also know of relevant individuals or companies locally. Within the education department you will find subject advisers who are familiar with resources for particular age ranges and subject areas.

Distribution

Most of your other print material will be sent out on request or to people known to you – on your database. Schools, though, might be a relatively new audience for your charity.

There are various ways of reaching schools. You might focus on your local area and make personal calls, you might work through relevant educational advisers based in your local authority. But if you want to reach a wider audience, you will need to do a combination of direct mail and PR. There are a number of education mailing houses offering opportunities to contact primary, secondary, special schools, different colleges, etc. This is probably the cheapest and easiest way of reaching them.

Education mailing houses offer a wide range of services. You can supply them with the appropriate number of fliers for distribution. But they can print the promotional leaflets for you. In some cases you can book what's known as a 'shared mailing'. Your leaflet is sent out with about nine others. This is cheaper than a 'solo mailing' where your flier is sent on its own. You can also buy mailing labels and details on disc, but this option is usually more expensive. *The Education Yearbook* lists relevant mailing houses and details are included in the final chapter of this book.

Annual reports

Annual reports and reviews can be very straightforward financial summaries with a few comments from key people in the organisation. These will be lodged with the relevant authorities and copies circulated to a limited number of people.

Alternatively, you might see the annual report as an opportunity to promote your charity to anyone who has been involved, or who shows an interest. In this case, you will want to go for higher quality production and offer your reader more information about achievements in the past year and plans for the coming one.

Content

All annual reports and accounts contain the legally required financial information plus reports from relevant individuals or committees. There are explanatory notes to the accounts, and a report from the auditors. This information is interesting and necessary, but it needn't be all that is included.

Case studies or project reports from your charity's work over the past year can bring your annual report to life and show the value of your organisation, especially when illustrated with photographs.

You might also use the annual report to look forward, describing how particular project funding will be spent, and any proposed changes to the work you're doing. This will help readers to feel involved and informed.

You could include a section in the report on planned projects in need of further funding. The annual report provides a good setting for this, because you are demonstrating your accountability and good management in the document.

Marketing opportunities

If you have produced a high quality annual report, then you will want to distribute it effectively. You might send copies out with a general covering letter to a number of your contacts. Some supporters and donors might appreciate an individual letter with a note about something in the report that should be of particular interest.

Contributions

Your annual report doesn't have to be written by one person. You might invite client, member or supporter contributions to bring in different voices.

Think of the different impact of the following types of contribution:

'This year we provided 300 children with books and toys donated by other families.'

'I couldn't even keep up with the rent. I felt so guilty. But Tom made do with a ball and a teddy. Then I found out about the Toy "n" Book Cupboard... it sounds silly but it's changed our lives. I've taught Tom to read and he's never short of toys now. He still loves his teddy though!'

CASE STUDY

United Response in its 1998 annual report includes comments and contributions from:

- its patron, The Duchess of Kent;
- its president, Martyn Lewis CBE;
- its chief executive, Sue Sayer;

- individual service users and families – their personal stories.

The charity takes the opportunity to describe its services and support in more detail. The cover of the report has a flap allowing additional leaflets to be inserted.

L'Arche UK uses a flap in the back cover of its annual report as a tear-off reply slip – it can be used to request more information or to accompany a donation. As well as including quotes from service users and staff, it includes a comment from a clinical psychologist who gives 'a professional view from the outside.'
· · · · · · · · ·

Newsletters
· · · · · · · · ·

Newsletters come in all shapes and sizes (and we'll look at some of the options below). They can help you to achieve a number of things, including:

- keeping staff, volunteers and clients informed about your various projects and activities – so that they know what is going on and can give out accurate information to anyone who enquires;

- keeping funders informed about how their contributions are helping your work – so that they feel positive about their investment and can justify their funding to their management or shareholders;

- motivating staff and volunteers – this might be fairly general in that they will see how well the charity is doing as a whole; it might be more specific if you write about their particular work;

- attracting repeat funding or new funders – by demonstrating how well you use donors' money you should attract more;

- promoting projects and services – people will be in touch with your charity for a particular reason, they might not know about the range of your work;

- celebrating success and sharing good practice – you can give people and projects the recognition they deserve and tell others about some of the things you've learnt in the process;

- offering an 'added value' service to clients and customers.

Your audience

We have already seen that a newsletter can help you to do a variety of things, for many different people. So your audience is likely to include:

- staff and/or volunteers;
- clients/users (and their families and friends);
- potential clients/users;
- funders/donors.

You might produce different newsletters for different audiences. You might produce one newsletter for all. If you do produce an all-purpose newsletter then it's important to remember every different member of your audience – considering their interests and needs. Someone producing a newsletter, for instance, for both the medical profession and clients would avoid technical jargon. Someone producing a newsletter for funders and staff would probably not draw attention to a project which had failed to work out.

Format and layout

If you are designing a newsletter for the first time, it is a good idea to look at some of the different approaches used by other charities. Don't get distracted by the degree of glossiness (and the likely cost) at this stage. Focus on the size and impact. Discover what you like and what seems appropriate to your own organisation's needs first.

Size

The main options are:

- A4 (the size of a normal letter);
- A5 (half the size of a normal letter);
- A3 (twice the size of a normal letter and about the size of a tabloid newspaper).

Many organisations opt for the A 3 size. It means you can use quite large print, so it's easier to read, and helps the newsletter 'feel' different from day to day correspondence which is generally A4. And in just four pages you can pack in quite a lot of information.

The A4 and A 5 options might be easier to produce than A 3 if you are going to run them off on your own computer. If you have fewer stories to include you might want to go for one of the smaller sizes.

A4 is also more appropriate if you are going for a large number of pages – particularly if you bring out your newsletter quarterly or twice a year.

Number of pages

When you have decided on the size you want to use, you then need to decide on the number of pages. There are various reasons for keeping the number of pages fairly low, including:

- Reader's time – this is nearly always limited, no matter how committed and interested they are. Get across a few important messages, don't bury them in a mass of information.

- Your time – compiling a newsletter with fewer pages and fewer stories will take you less time to pull together.

- Production costs – fewer pages means the newsletter will be less expensive to produce.

- Postage costs – a lighter newsletter will cost less to mail out.

- Storage space – fewer pages means the newsletters take up less room when they're in your building.

- Environmental impact – fewer pages means less paper is used in the process.

Most newsletters will be four to eight sides (pages) in total. Some will be a double-sided single sheet of paper (more of a bulletin than a newsletter).

You can, of course, always vary the number of pages if you have a particularly busy period or lots of important news. But it helps with planning and budgeting to stick to a standard number for most issues.

Having said that, if you are producing fewer issues of your newsletter then you should probably include more pages. This is particularly true if you produce a publication for a large membership. The Downs Syndrome Association, for instance, produces a seasonal newsletter of 40 pages. It is full of news and features, photographs and letters.

Masthead and contents list

Newsletters usually have mastheads. Just as with newspapers, your reader should be able to identify your newsletter by the title, logo and design work at the top of page one. Often some sort of thick line or strip is used with the title above, or part of, this line. The line helps to draw the eye to the top of the page. It also clearly distinguishes the branding from the main stories within the newsletter itself.

The elements which you might incorporate into your masthead include:

- your logo;
- the name of your organisation;
- the title of your newsletter (two to three words maximum);
- the issue number;
- the issue date;
- the price (if there is one).

You will probably also have a contents list on page one. Even with four page newsletters it is important to draw the reader in. The contents list or box doesn't give a full run-down on all the stories. It's more of a tease or promotion for some of the important articles.

Columns

The masthead goes right across the top of the page. But individual articles generally run down columns. This is because the eye tires if it has to read right across the page. And you want to hold your readers' attention.

The standard is to use two or three columns on a sheet of A4. A sheet of A3 would probably have five or six columns.

Columns don't have to constrain you. Often the lead story will have an introductory paragraph which runs across two or more columns in a larger typeface (often also in bold type). Then subsequent paragraphs run in the standard columns.

Other main articles may follow a similar style. Smaller stories of just one or two paragraphs might run entirely over two columns).

Columns are guidelines that help to give a shape to the overall page.

Fonts

You have a wide choice of fonts to use in your newsletter. You might want to use a font that your organisation already uses in other materials. You might want to go for something different.

You can use two or three fonts throughout the newsletter – having a main font for articles, a font for headlines and another for captions. Go for fonts that are clear and plain, rather than twiddly ones that are hard to read. You can use serif or sans serif fonts as long as they have lots of white space (leading) and are simple to read.

Headlines

We return to headlines in the 'content' section on page 50 and talk about the kind of words to use. Here we are concerned with how the headlines appear.

Headlines can run over one or more lines. Generally they should fill up the available width with no white space left over.

You should establish a set of rules on the typesizes you use. You might for instance have different sizes allocated to the following:

- main story, front page;
- centre spread (across two inside pages);
- back page lead story;
- important articles;
- minor articles.

Intro

Underneath your heading and before the article begins you might include an 'intro'. This is a one sentence summary which intrigues and entices the reader to read on. Under the headline 'Hamlet Cries Foul' you might find the intro 'Something is rotten in the state of Denmark . . .' This intro is normally in italics and is in a larger typeface than the opening paragraph.

Sub-heads (cross-heads)

There are further devices to attract the reader and hold their interest. One of these is the sub or cross-head. One or two words are used to break up an article and reflect the contents of what follows. They are usually quite pointed words, words with many associations – anything from 'valuable' and 'crisis' to 'pickled' and 'tremendous'. Tabloid newspapers take the opportunity to use saucy words (probably inappropriate for your charity!)

The sub-head is usually in bold or in capital letters. It is in a larger type than the main body of the article.

By-lines

Different articles might be contributed by different individuals. In this case you might want to give them by-lines, that is an acknowledgment for the author. You can choose either to simply have 'by John Smith' in bold underneath the main heading, or you can incorporate the by-line into your intro... 'Something is rotten in the state of Denmark, as John Smith discovered'. It is important to establish a general rule for by-lines so that your contributors feel happy that they get due recognition.

If one person is writing the entire newsletter, then they shouldn't get by-lines all over the place. They might have a by-line on the lead article. More usually they would get a credit inside or at the end of the newsletter. An editor should be credited separately, rather than by-lined.

Captions

Picture captions need a standard style. Usually they are in smaller type than the rest of the newsletter. Often they are in italics and sometimes have a bullet point or symbol at the beginning.

Publishing details

Somewhere within your newsletter you should incorporate details of who has produced it. You might list writers, editors, etc. You should definitely give your contact details and charity number. It is quite common for this information to appear at the foot of the final page. Alternatively it might be placed in the top left hand corner of the second page.

Pictures and left to right design

One final point on design is to remember that we read from left to right, from top to bottom. If you are putting pictures onto a page it's important to remember this so that you don't cut a story in half.

A picture can go above a block of text (see Fig 3) or at the end of it (see Fig 4). It can also go in the middle of text if you wrap words around it so that the reader continues to read on (see Fig 5). But if you cut a column in half with a picture the reader won't make the leap to the remaining text below (see Fig 6). If you put a picture at the top of the middle column this also makes life difficult for the reader (see Fig 7). They will naturally look at the same level or below the start of the previous column. It takes extra effort to stretch back up the page.

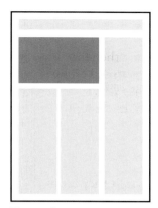

Figure 3

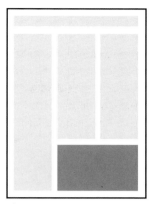

Figure 4

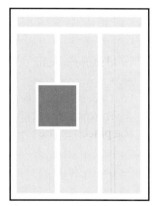

Figure 5

Figure 6

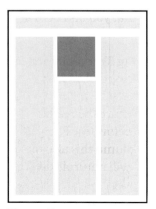

Figure 7

Content

Now we turn to the actual content of the newsletter. First, we will look at what you might include. Then we will talk about tips for style. Finally, we run through headline writing.

What to include

Your entire newsletter could be made up of news articles. You might include several major stories, some smaller stories and then various news-in-briefs (NIBs).

Another approach is to have the more newsy articles on the first and final pages. The centre pages then have features. These can be lighter in tone with plenty of pictures. On the other hand, they might be more analytical.

You aren't, though, limited to news stories, and features. You can also include letters from readers; real life stories; puzzles and competitions; tips and reader suggestions; an events diary, etc.

Let's look at these in more detail.

News stories

News should be quite current – although it depends on how regularly you bring out each edition. It should be something that doesn't happen very often and that makes people sit up and take notice.

Newsletters usually present very positive stories of up to around 500 words. They might highlight some of the challenges a project or person faced. But the outcome will usually be success and achievement – that's why you've chosen to feature it.

News stories work best when they include personal elements. Quotes from some of the people affected help to illustrate the power of a project, for instance. You can include value judgements much more comfortably if you are quoting someone. They can obviously give their opinion. It's an opportunity to include praise for the work you do without sounding as if you are just writing a puff piece.

If you are including quotes from people then it is very important to check that they are happy with what you are attributing to them. You don't have to repeat what they said verbatim. You can make it more succinct and you can even create new things for them. As long as you check that they are happy to be quoted as saying these things that's fine.

Features

Feature articles are more in-depth pieces. The longer news story is around 500 words, whereas a feature is probably 1,000 words or more. The two main types of features are at very different ends of the 'seriousness spectrum'. At one end there is the light report on a major event, with lots of pictures and different people's points of view. At the other end there is the detailed report on medical research and the analysis of legislation.

The more detailed analytical report will usually be contributed by a relevant professional or commentator. If the person is from outside your organisation then they might want to be paid for their time.

You might want to include a disclaimer at the end of the article to make it clear that the views expressed are those of the author and not necessarily your organisation's.

Sometimes two feature articles are included presenting differing and even opposing views. It's up to the reader to make up their mind which perspective they support.

Letters from readers

Readers' letters work well if you have a large membership to draw on, guaranteeing a regular flow of letters. If there aren't many potential letter-writers it can be a struggle to make this a regular part of your newsletter. Don't forget, however, that you need to invite readers to write in!

The often controversial, debating style of letters is interesting if your newsletter comes out weekly or monthly. But it's hard for readers to remember the last issue's hot topic three month's later.

Letters of thanks or appreciation can be worth including. They might refer to previous articles or to a specific project. It is important that any such letters are published because they will be of interest to others and not just as a piece of self-congratulation.

If you have received a number of letters on the same subject you might summarise them in one general piece. This could be an article saying 'we have received many letters in support of...' Or you might 'manufacture' a letter containing the main points made in a number of contributions.

It is worth checking back with the author of the letter before printing it to ensure that the letter is genuinely from them. Also check whether they want to give any contact details or to be anonymous.

Real life stories

True stories from readers can be very effective in attracting people to read your newsletter. Such personal stories can be moving: they can help other service users; and they capture what your organisation is all about. If you want to edit such a contribution then work with the contributor and ensure they are happy with your changes before going to print.

Real life stories might be contributed by the families of a service user. They might be written by a client of your organisation. Such stories would probably be directly relevant to the work of your charity. On the other hand you might ask someone connected with your charity to write about a personal experience in a completely different arena.

Puzzles and competitions

The quiz, cartoon and crossword areas in a newsletter can be appropriate if you are serving quite a diverse audience. They might attract some people to dip into the newsletter who otherwise wouldn't.

They can also be useful devices to find out more about your readers – you can run competitions that have quite detailed entry forms, for instance asking for a reader's post code, age, and interests.

You might want to run a sponsored competition. The sponsor would provide the prize and get due recognition within your newsletter. At the same time readers would have the opportunity to compete for a high value prize.

If you want to run a competition it is worth finding out from the Charity Commission whether or not your plans are acceptable. The Charity Commission is on 01823-345000.

Tips and reader suggestions

You might not be able to sustain a letters page where readers exchange views. But you might be able to include tips and suggestions. Families might make suggestions which help others. Project workers might share good practice ideas.

Events diary

The newsletter is a good place to publicise forthcoming events. These might be your own organisation's events, they might be events organised externally that are of interest.

Style

Newsletters should be written in simple English. Use short sentences, and write as you speak. Don't be afraid to start sentences with 'But' and 'And', it all helps the text to flow and makes it more comfortable for the reader. As with the design, you are trying to attract and hold readers' attention.

Stories should be structured in the same way as newspaper reports. When newspapers fit stories into the available space they cut them from the bottom. You should be able to take a similar approach with your newsletter. So, compose your stories with the most important information first and the least important last. Imagine the shape of your story as an upside down pyramid.

In fact, your story should make sense even if you only print the first paragraph which gives the essential details.

The first few paragraphs should answer

- who?
- what?
- why?
- where?
- when?
- and how?

in the relevant order.

It is good to include a human element – so quote some of the people involved. Make sure they are happy with the quote and how it will be used.

Headlines

Headlines can make a big difference to a newsletter. Again, they play a vital role in attracting attention and getting a reader to dip into the story. Writing headlines isn't easy, so here are a few tips to help you:

- use simple, punchy one/two-syllable words;
- use active doing-words in the present tense;
- avoid humour – not everyone finds the same things funny;
- try to capture the essence of the story;
- don't try to be too clever!

Photography

Strong pictures can transform a newsletter. They really can say much more than words. You might use images that are fun, artistic or moving. Feature people where you can – involved in the work of your organisation.

It is important to build up a file of photos you can use; otherwise you might be forced to choose between one or two badly taken snaps. Try to build a photographic record into all of your project plans. File them carefully so that you can find them again easily.

You won't be able to bring in a professional photographer each time. However, you probably will know someone who is a keen amateur photographer. Alternatively you might invest in a high quality camera and some basic training for a member of your team.

Even if your newsletter is in black and white or two-colour it is worth taking a photograph in colour. Colour photos can be reproduced in black and white, and at the same time you will have high quality colour photos to use in other materials.

Try to avoid line ups where people are simply shaking hands – the 'grab and grin' approach. If possible, capture people in action, enjoying themselves and unaware of the camera.

The photographs will usually be scanned in by your designer. They can also be scanned in at a later stage by the company printing your newsletter. Most scanners are able to reproduce images from both slides and prints. The most important thing is that the photograph should be crisp and clear.

Once scanned, the photographs can then be made larger or smaller to fit the appropriate space. They can also be 'cropped' – cutting out inappropriate elements from the edges (large bits of sky, etc.), thus focusing in on the main players.

It is important to keep track of the photos you use – labelling them clearly for designers and printers, and returning them to their owners afterwards or filing them for future use. When labelling them carefully place a pre-written label on the back of prints or on the edges of slides. Do not write directly on the back of a photograph as this will damage the image.

Be careful not to offend anyone by printing a photo of them without their permission or by giving their picture a misleading caption.

Timetables

Many organisations produce newsletters. Fewer issue regular newsletters. A production timetable will help you ensure that your quarterly newsletter doesn't become a twice-yearly publication. It will also help you to involve other people, in turn giving them specific deadlines.

Your timetable should include the following steps:

- review previous edition and note any amendments/improvements;
- draw up table of contents;
- commission articles from contributors – with guidelines, brief and deadline;
- research and write other articles;
- collate pictures/take new pictures as necessary;
- edit contributions and check quotes, etc.;
- prioritise stories, decide design layout and further edit as necessary;
- write headlines, sub-heads, captions, etc.;
- proof read/sign off;
- print;
- distribute.

It is worth putting together a timetable across the next 12 months which shows the dates of the above steps for each edition. After issuing a newsletter you might want to amend and extend your timetable.

Advertisers

Newsletters can be fairly expensive to produce. You might want to offset some or all of the costs through advertising.

If you decide to do this you will need to draw up a rate card which sets out the costs of advertisements in your newsletter according to their size and position.

When you are considering how much to charge people think about the amount of time one of your team could spend on selling the space. You might want to increase the price of adverts accordingly. If an organisation wants to buy a batch of adverts over a number of editions you can then give them a discount because less time will be spent selling.

CASE STUDY
·········

A national fundraising organisation produces a monthly A4 newsletter for nearly 4,000 members. The current rates for black and white adverts are £315 for a quarter page advert, £495 for a half page and £895 for a full page.

By contrast a county-wide carers group produces a quarterly A5 newsletter. Half page black and white adverts cost £100 and full page adverts cost £175. If adverts are booked across four editions there is a 10 per cent discount.
·········

Ask advertisers to supply their adverts to you if possible. Tell them the format you want: on disc, in a particular software package; on paper, black and white or colour, etc. If the advert is supplied on disc ask them to provide a list of fonts they have used to make sure you have got them too. Send them a proof of how their advert will appear and ask them to sign it off. Spending a few minutes getting it checked is worth it to ensure your advertiser is happy. They will be more likely to buy further adverts in the future.

Visual aids
·········

As you go out and about promoting your organisation, speaking at events and making presentations to funders you will probably make use of visual aids in some shape or form.

These might be on-screen presentations (using a computer software package like Powerpoint) or they might take the form of overhead projections (OHPs). We have included visual aids in this section on printed materials, because if you use slides directly from your computer they will be quite similar to printed OHPs. The main difference is that instead of working with individual printed overheads, a separate projector and screen, you link your computer directly to a large screen.

All the slides in your computerised presentation are stored in one file. You open the file and click through the different pages with a mouse.

What appears on screen is usually higher quality than an overhead and it fills the whole screen.

Borders

Many people use borders on their overheads. In fact, most of the computer packages that help you design slides give you a selection to choose from. This is not just about drawing a pretty box for the sake of it. A border helps the audience to focus on the key information. It acts as a frame – the message is inside. Anything outside the frame is a distraction.

It is important to go for a simple border that is consistent in all slides. If you are over-elaborate then the audience will be looking at the wrong thing.

Fonts

Clean and simple fonts are most appropriate for slides. Lots of leading (white space) between the lines of type will make it easier for the audience to read.

Try to stick to a single font so that the slide doesn't look over-fussy.

Logos

When you make a presentation you have an opportunity to promote your organisation. You will be talking as an individual, but your slides can carry a reminder of the organisation you represent. The subtle use of a small logo within the border or in one of the corners of the slide will help to do this.

Many television stations now use a logo in this way. It almost becomes invisible and the viewer can concentrate on the action.

All the time, though, they are aware at some level of the channel they are tuned to.

Content

Slides and OHPs are there to enhance your presentation. They shouldn't be used as speaker's notes. And they definitely shouldn't be audience handouts.

All too often people put up an OHP with the headings of their talk and then leave that on screen as a prompt. If there are 27 headings up there, you can guarantee that your audience will be tense until you reach point 26.

Many speakers also cram too much detail on their OHPs – putting complicated graphs and lots of bullet points. Pie charts work well. Other graphs should be reproduced as handouts. Four bullet points are easy to read, five is pushing it. Rather than squeezing all relevant information onto one slide, move onto a second.

As with other materials, go for simple punchy words. Mnemonics work well and help people remember what you have said. For instance, a slide explaining how a rest home puts people at ease might say 'We greet people with our CAT – 'Come in, 'Ave a cup of tea, Take a seat'. Even very weak humour seems to work in this context!

Posters, adverts and fliers

Posters, adverts and fliers can be used to promote specific goods, services and events that you are offering. They might also be used more generally to promote your organisation as a whole. Adverts could, of course, be used to recruit new members of staff or volunteers.

Posters, adverts and fliers are trying to get your message across to either:

- complete strangers;

- people who have an interest in your work, but aren't expecting to receive any information.

There are a number of steps you will want them to go through. You need to:

1 grab their attention;

2 get their interest;

3 convince them of your message;

4 motivate them to act;

5 ensure they take action.

They need to work their way through all of these stages. If they don't make it to the final and fifth stage then they might feel good about you but do nothing about it. All is not lost if they get 'stuck' at an earlier stage. They might feel well disposed towards you next time you come back with a further promotional message.

Format

Let's look in turn at the formats you might use for posters, adverts and fliers.

Posters

Posters have to stand out from a distance. They might be vying with other literature on a wall. They might be standing alone on a large hoarding. Distinctive background colours can help to draw the eye. A white background will just get lost.

Large bold words work well. Sometimes, though, you might attract attention by using a few very small words or no words at all.

Adverts

Adverts can have a variety of dimensions – square, landscape, portrait, etc. You might need to design for these different shapes. Adverts can be large with lots of space for information. They might be a small box containing a few words only plus a phone number. It all depends on your budget and the publications in which your advert might appear. Always include clearly readable contact details and don't give a phone number unless someone – or a machine – is there to answer it.

Fliers

Fliers are usually A4 or smaller. They often feature a tear-off reply slip, sometimes with a reply-paid postcard. If you are going for a tear-off slip ensure the information on the reverse is non-essential or relevant to the reply. Include your contact details elsewhere within the flier so that the recipient has your details even if they send back the tear-off slip.

To arrange a freepost address and set up reply-paid postcards you should contact the Royal Mail Sales Centre on 0345-950950.

Content

When you are devising the content of your poster, advert, or flier then you might want to consider whether it helps people move through the five stages we saw earlier.

1 How are you going to grab their attention? Will you tease them or scream at them with words? Will you shock or intrigue them with an image?

2 How will you get their interest? Will you feature a compelling or personal message? Will you appeal to their emotions, needs or desires?

3 How will you convince them of your message? You need to 'sell' the quality and importance of what's on offer.

4 How will you motivate them to act? Usually a snappy summary of the benefits of their involvement is appropriate.

5 How will you ensure they take action? On a flier, a tear-off slip or pre-paid envelope makes life easy for them. A freephone telephone number on an advert or poster might prompt them to act. You might follow up with a door to door campaign.

A poster will need to condense all of the information you want to convey into as few words as possible. A flier can give much more detail. An advert might be a repeat of what is on a poster or might have a little more information. You don't have to choose one or other; you could use a combination of all of them, using one theme and design, but different degrees of information.

Postcards and greetings cards
· · · · · · · · ·

Postcards and greetings cards can be used to keep people informed of specific projects and to remind them of your existence.

You might send out postcards when a new service starts up, or to celebrate the completion of a project. Greetings cards will be sent out to mark particular festivals or awareness days.

In the main these cards are sent to people who are already in touch with your organisation and are, therefore, on your mailing list. However, they can also be used to raise awareness of a particular issue with a wider audience.

Postcards and greetings cards work by featuring a very strong image – one that people will want to keep and pin on their wall. They can be more abstract and obscure than other promotional material.

The reverse of the postcard is printed as any other, with space for an address on the right. Further details can be printed on the left hand side.

Greetings cards carry a message inside and your organisation's details on the back.

CASE STUDY
· · · · · · · · ·

The Health Education Authority has used postcards in a number of its awareness-raising campaigns. In 1997 it ran a postcard campaign as part of World Mental Health Day. Several different designs of postcard were used. Each featured a young person with a slogan such as 'loony', and 'nutter'. The postcards were sent to organisations which then circulated the postcards to their members. Many schools used the postcards to raise issues around the stigma associated with mental health problems.

··········

Exhibition panels
··········

If you attend exhibitions or fairs, if you give talks to schools and other groups, or if you run events, then you will probably want to have at least one set of exhibition panels.

If you are giving a talk then exhibition panels can provide your set or backdrop. As with slides which contain your organisation's logo, exhibition panels remind people that you represent a particular group. You get your branding across as people focus on you (and the panels) for the length of your presentation.

At exhibitions or fairs the panels need to work harder because they will be competing with other boards. They have to attract people over to your stand to find out more.

If you are running an event then well-designed panels help to reinforce your brand and give you ownership of the space even if you are in a hired building.

Format
···········

Exhibition panels can be purpose-built if you have quite a large budget. There are specialist companies which will design a unique set for you, store it when it's not in use, transport it and set it up for you at various venues. Such an approach is out of the reach of most organisations. So we will focus on off-the-shelf and lower budget options.

You might decide to create some mounted materials that can be velcro-ed onto boards – either owned by you or provided by a host organisation. There is quite a bit of flexibility in this approach. You can produce a number of different panels and then choose the most appropriate. You can go for different shapes, individual lettering, more unusual materials, etc. to illustrate your work. All can be stuck onto the boards.

You might go for straightforward large panels which fill each board. If possible go for slightly smaller dimensions so that you can use the panels on other shapes and sizes of boards.

The backing boards are usually blue, grey or maroon and they screw together in different ways. You can have a set of single boards on long legs (see Fig 8). You can also have a double row of boards with a narrow 'header' panel. If you go for this configuration you will usually have at least eight large boards in total so that four central boards form the main backdrop with two boards acting as supporting 'wings' on each side (see Fig 9).

Another alternative is to use panels inserted into a folding metal framework. These usually come in sets of eight large panels which fold out in a similar way to the boards described above. You can also fit a header and lights to the framework. This model usually requires additional backer panels – they can be blank or feature a design so that the entire exhibition is reversible (see Fig 10).

The other main style of exhibition panel uses tall plastic banners with magnetic strips. These are hung from a metal mesh which unfolds and expands to two or three metres high. Four long banners form a semi-circular display with two small curved end panels (see Fig 11).

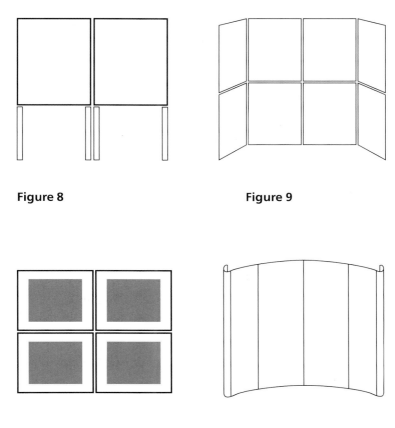

Figure 8

Figure 9

Figure 10

Figure 11

Content

In the main, exhibition panels need to make an impact with large clear images and words. On some occasions you might want to have more detailed written information if a stand is unstaffed. Usually, though, the stand's purpose is to attract people to you; staff or volunteers will be on hand to give out the information.

Big bold logos, striking pictures and enticing slogans do this sort of work.

Bright colours also help to attract attention. And it is worth using spotlights to highlight appropriate sections of the display.

Production

How your exhibition panels are produced will depend on the type of boards you are using. If you are going for velcro-ed attachments then you might print onto paper or card which is then mounted onto a thicker panel. You can also have shapes carved out of foam or polystyrene materials. It is possible to buy the materials from a DIY or artstore. However, most organisations commission an audio visual or exhibition company to produce these cut outs.

The panels which are inserted into metal frames and the plastic hanging banners are specially printed and sealed. Most designers will be able to find an appropriate printer/production company on your behalf.

Certificates

Certificates are usually presented to people or organisations in recognition of their achievements or to acknowledge that they are members of a particular organisation.

You might have a membership scheme for young people, for instance. Sending the members a certificate acts as a constant reminder of their involvement and helps to keep them in contact.

Rewarding someone for their achievements with a certificate means they feel recognised for their contribution. At the same time they hang the certificate in pride of place, helping to promote your organisation further.

Format

Certificates are usually A4 in size – this ensures they have the right degree of impact and can be seen from a short distance.

Commonly they have a frame or border, and they are usually produced on a high quality stock of paper or card.

Content

Your logo and name will usually feature prominently at the head of the certificate. Then the name of the recipient will be included – usually in the middle of a statement about why they have been awarded the certificate. And a senior representative of your organisation usually signs the certificate to add status.

Internal documents

The final focus of this section is on internal documents. You might not consider these as candidates for 'promotional material', but they do have an important role in developing a united approach to your image.

The need for internal consistency

Earlier we talked about the danger of different individuals and departments producing material to different designs and standards. If you want to encourage a 'corporate' approach to the use of your logo and branding then this should be carried through in internal documents.

You can issue branding guidelines, but there's nothing like demonstrating these rules in action.

Internal printed documents are issued more frequently than external ones. Memos and notices will be on or near the desks of your staff and volunteers who will see them almost every day, giving you a great opportunity to advertise your new approach to the look and feel of your organisation.

Memos, notices, manuals

Each organisation will have different internal documents. Some of the main ones, though, are memos, notices/bulletins and manuals/staff handbooks.

Memos can follow through on the design you have used for your fax header – creating a black and white version of your letterhead with appropriate details of who has issued it and to whom it is being circulated.

Notices which are displayed in public places might be seen by people from outside the organisation. Keep them friendly and in house style – not scrappy hand-written photocopies.

Manuals are important because they might be a person's first main introduction to the organisation. From their initial interview and through the induction process you can issue materials to them which reinforce the organisation's branding.

It's not indoctrination, it's about developing a professional culture and a united message.

Accessibility

When you are producing printed materials you need to make them accessible to the potential audience. In some cases this might mean producing an audio cassette version – in English or other languages. We look at this in more detail in Chapter 5.

You might produce large print versions of your leaflets. Some materials might be made available in Braille. The RNIB (see Further Help) can advise you on how to produce materials appropriately for visually impaired people.

CASE STUDY

The RNIB worked with the Meridian Broadcasting Trust to produce a Braille promotion on the cover of an information booklet for visually impaired people and their families. The booklet itself was in large print. The back cover had a message in Braille saying how to obtain a Braille version.

If you are producing materials for people with learning difficulties then you might want to develop picture/symbol-based versions. The Makaton Vocabulary Development Project has done a lot of work in this area.

CHAPTER FOUR

Working with designers and printers

This section looks at some of the ways you can work effectively with designers and printers. Even if you are using people within your own organisation problems can arise if you are working with different priorities, standards and workloads.

Staff, volunteers, students or professionals?

Everyone has their own opinion on design. They know what they like and what they don't like. They might not always know why, though.

You might be lucky and have a member of staff, a volunteer or a student placement who has design skills. However, if design isn't the main focus of their work then it might still be advisable to work with a professional agency. Otherwise you run the risk of the design work being pushed to one side because of the other pressures on your colleague's time. Design is not something that should be fitted in around other work.

An external designer will be able to devote their attention and energy to working on your project. In addition, as a full-time designer they will be in touch with the latest trends and technology. And they will be able to offer you a range of creative solutions to choose from.

If you decide to work with an external designer – either an individual freelance or a company – then you will first want to select an appropriate one. You might find an agency in a variety of ways, including:

- through recommendation by a contact, colleague or friend;
- by seeing a piece of work you like and finding out who worked on it;
- by looking up a number of companies in a directory and inviting them to send in samples of their work.

It is vital that you have a good personal rapport with your preferred designer because you need to work closely together and they need to understand your thinking. They also need a thorough understanding of your organisation if they are to capture its personality in their design work.

Getting quotes

When you are deciding on who to work with, you will need to consider their fees.

Design quotes

Some design agencies want to charge a fee when they pitch for work if they are asked to develop some new visuals. This is understandable as it involves them in quite a bit of preparation time. If you think this is too expensive an option then you should ask to see samples of their existing work. Then you simply pay the designer of your choice when they are working on your particular design job.

Print quotes

At the same time as getting quotes for the design work you might want to get quotes for the printing of the materials.

You can either go through the design agency (who will usually add a print management fee) or you can work directly with the printers. If you choose to work directly with the printers you need to allow yourself time to meet them, check work in progress and ensure they meet your deadlines.

Sometimes it is simpler to work through the designers. The designer can often get better deals from the printer because they work regularly with them. The discount often covers the designer's print management fee, so you end up getting the designer's input at no extra cost.

Drawing up a specification

Whether you are getting a quote directly from a printer, or going through a designer the printer will need a detailed specification for your print requirements so that they can provide an accurate quote. The designer should advise you on issues such as the weight of paper and other technical details.

The more detailed you can be the more easily you can compare quotes – you will be comparing like with like. And you have to decide on these issues eventually when the job goes off to be printed, so you might as well decide on the specification at this stage.

Usually you will need to give clear instructions about:

- Number of pages – (remember to include the cover in your calculations – and consider whether any text will appear on the inside front or back covers).

- Any special cutting requirements – (eg folders with tailored pockets: these are flaps which are cut to an unusual shape, meaning that a printer has to order them to be specially made which adds to the time and cost involved).

- Number of colours – (and any 'special' colours that aren't made up from the four-colour process – see the paragraph following).

- Weight (or weights) of paper – (usually given in gsm. Standard laser printer/photocopier paper is 80gsm. An A4 information booklet or annual report would usually use 100–125gsm for the main text pages. Newsletters and fliers are usually printed on 115gsm or more. Booklet covers tend to be between 175 and 250gsm).

- Environmental requirements – (recycled fibre content, etc.).

- Print run and any run on quote required – (the print run refers to the number of copies required. As you produce more copies the unit cost comes down. So you might decide to print 2,000 copies at 50p a copy rather than 500 at £1 per copy. The run on quote is how much the printer would charge for an additional number of copies produced at the same time. This can help you to decide whether to ask for 3,000 copies, 3,500 or 4,000, for instance).

- How any text will be supplied – (eg on disc or by e-mail).

- Number of photographs to be supplied – (and in what format).

- Any illustrations required – (and the number per page).

- Whether you want materials to be sealed or laminated – (when print is sealed the ink is prevented from rubbing off on the readers' hands. Laminating makes print stainproof, stiffer and brighter. You can go for a matt or gloss finish. Lamination makes print harder to recycle).

- Proofs/cromalins required for checking purposes – (proofs are laser printed outputs of your work and are useful for checking the way the material is laid out and the content. They are usually produced by the designer. Cromalins are produced by the printer and are usually supplied in colour on fairly thick shiny paper. They give you a fair idea of how each page will looked when printed).

- Timetable/deadline.

- Delivery details.

When deciding on the colours to use it might be worth considering how a lot of colour printing is done by mixing together the colours black, cyan, magenta and yellow. This allows the printer to create most colours and reproduce colour photographs. Special colours are those which can't be created by combining the four, thus creating the need for additional inks to be used. A special is often needed for logos with distinctive shades.

Printers will advise you if there is anything else they need to know about a particular piece of work. Digital printing means that you can now print small runs of documents relatively cheaply.

Design and print specification for a newsletter

Number of pages: 4

Colours: 2 – black and bright green (pantone reference 360)

Weight of paper: 115 gsm

Recycled fibre content: 100 per cent

Print run: 1,000 (500 run on)

Text supplied: e-mail

Photographs: 8 total, supplied as black and white prints

Illustrations: none

Treatment: sealed

Timetable: text delivered on xx, laser proofs required on yy

Delivery: to address on zz

Briefing and developing ideas

Whether you are using an 'in-house' designer or someone from outside you will need to brief them clearly.

First, it's important to meet them to explain more about your work and what you are trying to achieve with the design. Show them as much of your existing material as possible explaining what you like and don't like. Ask them for some initial ideas to check that they understand what you are trying to get at.

Look at some of their work and say what you like and how things might be adapted to suit what you are doing. This will help them because you are talking in concrete terms, and in terms which are meaningful to them. Also point out anything you don't like so that you prevent them using this approach on your work.

The formal design brief

Once you are comfortable with the design agency you should run through the specifics of what you want them to do. This could be an entirely new approach for all of your materials, what's known as a 'corporate redesign'. Alternatively you might want them to work on a single leaflet. Either way you need to give them a formal written brief.

A brief should cover:

- the purpose of the materials they are working on;
- the audience for these materials;
- their contact point in your organisation;
- the approval process;
- your requirements.

Sample brief

You are designing a quarterly newsletter for the Directory Recycling Project. Below we provide further information about the newsletter to assist with design issues.

- The newsletter is issued to raise awareness of general recycling issues, and to provide updates on the activities of the Directory Recycling Project. It also gives information on how interested parties can become involved in collection and recycling schemes and receive financial and practical support from the project. The newsletter needs to grab attention and stimulate people to participate.

- The audience for the newsletter is primarily local authority recycling officers. In addition it will be read by community recyclers, commercial recycling organisations and trade journalists.

- Copy will be supplied on disc by James Ryman. James will also provide colour photographs. For further information, and editing of articles to fit available space please liaise with James.

- Drafts should be submitted to Sarah Jones for comment. A final approval copy should be supplied with a written confirmation form.
- The print specification (see above).

Proofing

Most print for leaflets, brochures, reports and so on is now drafted by the client and supplied on computer disc to the designer. In the past, type or hand-written material had to be typeset by a third party. When this was the case proof-reading played a very important part of the design process because all the text had been re-keyed. Today, most of the rigorous proof-reading of text should be done before the disc is given to the designer. Some designers charge for every correction that is made. Others charge for the time involved. So the cleaner the copy (your text) when you hand it over the better.

There is still a need to proof the material once the designer has laid it out on the page. Sometimes it's easier to spot a mistake when it is displayed in a different way. One last read-through might help you to simplify the wording and make a big improvement. Also, designers move text around as they fit it into the space available and they might erase or re-type some words – spelling mistakes can creep in. They might paste the wrong bit of text into a particular position or use the wrong picture caption.

If you are producing a lot of materials in this way, it could be worth training a member of staff in proof-reading. A number of cost-effective courses are available.

No matter how many times you proof-read something you will always be able to think of ways to improve it or even spot a silly mistake once it's printed. It might be worth bringing in a second fresh pair of eyes to read it through before you agree to go ahead and print.

Sign-off

Most designers will ask you to sign and date the approved design before it is printed. Usually you will be signing-off a laser proof, either in black and white or colour depending on the job. Two further checks can be made, though, and these are:

1 A colour proof – which your designers run off on their desk top printer so that you can check that you are generally happy with how it feels in colour.

2 A cromalin – which the printer produces giving you an accurate picture of how the finished product will look (sometimes it looks glossier than the final version).

Delivery, storage and distribution

The production process doesn't end when you give the go-ahead for printing. You need to make arrangements for the delivery of the materials to one or more destinations.

You might need to book storage space. It's worth considering that 10,000 A4 fliers would take up the same amount of room as the average single bed and 5,000 A3 annual reports could take up four times this amount of room. If you don't have sufficient room for these then you might be able to make arrangements with a sponsor or with a neighbouring building. If not, then there are storage companies charging quite small sums of money for up to 20 bankers boxes full of material. They are listed in *Yellow Pages*.

You might need to make arrangements for onward distribution.

CASE STUDY

A Wiltshire-based youth arts charity produced 5,000 fliers and distributed almost all the copies to libraries, youth and community centres, pubs and similar venues. The local authorities helped to distribute batches of leaflets to libraries and youth centres. However, the charity itself had to load up a van and visit the other venues individually to hand over the fliers.

CHAPTER FIVE

Audio

There are a number of reasons why you might use audio cassettes to help promote your organisation.

Audio cassettes enable you to reach people who might not be able to read your printed materials easily, such as:

- visually impaired people;
- people with literacy difficulties;
- children;
- people with learning disabilities.

Many charities feel that it's important to produce materials in this way – even if they are not directly connected with one of these beneficiary groups.

CASE STUDY

The Alzheimer's Disease Society, for instance, has produced several audio cassette versions of its leaflets for visually impaired people who have been personally affected by Alzheimer's Disease. The society has also produced introductory tapes in Polish, Hindi and Cantonese. This allows the society to extend its support services to a wider audience.
· · · · · · · · ·

Equally, audio cassettes allow you to make a different style of promotional material: clients, volunteers and others can speak directly to the listener. They can engage them with their personal experiences.

The listener can use their imagination, yet also be captivated by what they hear. It's a very direct way of reaching people and ensuring they take in some of your message.

There are two main types of audio cassettes you could produce. The first is known as a 'talking book' – where the printed version is simply read out and recorded. The second is a specially produced tape, like a radio programme. A script is developed and interviews conducted with relevant people.

We look in further detail at these two options below.

Talking books

Talking books transfer your written material onto tape. To do this you could use a member of your team with a good voice and hire a small recording studio for half a day. Alternatively you might hire some equipment and use a quiet or soundproof building of your own. This way you can spend longer on the recording and perhaps tape a few different brochures, newsletters, etc. at the same time.

You might want to pay a local Talking Newspaper group to record the material for you in their soundproof facilities. Their volunteers regularly put material onto tape, so they can guarantee the good results that might not be easily achievable on your own. The costs are a matter for you to negotiate with your local organisation, but are relatively low – usually based on the number of hours involved in the production. The Talking Newspaper Association of the United Kingdom (TNAUK) can give you further information (ring 01435-866102).

When you are recording printed materials, it's worth considering whether or not you need to edit them or adapt them in some way. This is particularly true of long lists or directories. Remember that not everything that reads well on paper sounds good when read out loud.

It might be more appropriate to give an overview of a directory and refer people to a telephone number for further details. If the original print contains illustrations you might need to find a way of conveying this information.

CASE STUDY

A Scottish health charity produced an audio cassette on alcohol misuse for young visually impaired people. The original leaflet included a diagram with arrows showing the route taken by alcohol in the bloodstream. In the audio tape the commentator said: 'there is a drawing of a young person taking a drink. Arrows show how the alcohol moves through the body . . .' Instead of a directory of helpful numbers, the cassette includes one single phone number. The helpline staff have details of the other appropriate numbers and can help to signpost the caller to the relevant organisation.

Once you have these talking book versions of your material it's easy to put them on the shelf and wait for people to ask for them. However, the potential audience might not realise that the tapes are available. It's a good idea to promote their availability by putting a large print note on the written version or by asking people which format they prefer when they order materials.

You can display them in a prominent position in your building/s so that clients, staff and volunteers know they are available.

Tailor-made cassettes

If you want to produce a specially-created audio cassette then you probably need to work with a media production company or freelance radio journalist/producer.

Selecting a producer

As with all contracts you should invite more than one individual or organisation to pitch for the work. This enables you to be sure you are getting value for money, and the most appropriate creative approach.

You can find potential production companies through the IVCA handbook and *The White Book* (see Further Help). Individual freelances are listed in the *NUJ Freelance Directory*. Word of mouth recommendations are worth following up. Local producers are also listed in the *Yellow Pages*.

You should provide the tenderers with a brief, outlining:

- the purpose of the cassette;
- your target audience;
- how the tape will be used;
- the length of the tape you want;
- the mix of interviews and locations you want;
- the need for voice over/reporter;
- the need for music;
- a timetable for production;
- the number of tapes you want.

You can ask the bidders to provide a quote covering all of the above, or you might ask them to quote for the provision of a master and sub-master tape which you will duplicate. You can also ask them for a rough outline of their approach and for samples of previous work.

You will probably use a variety of criteria in making your decision – from price to appropriate style and ideas.

The production process

Once you have selected the producer then you should give them a more thorough briefing which honestly outlines any potential problems and goes to the heart of what you want to achieve.

You will probably also negotiate with them on price.

The producer will provide a more detailed outline of their approach and a production timetable. And you can be more or less involved as things progress. You will definitely be involved in checking draft scripts, approving decisions on potential interviewees and other participants. You might help to introduce the producer to relevant people or you might leave it up to them to make contact. It all depends on the level of trust you have in them, your need or desire to be involved and the time you have available.

There is no single correct or preferred approach. There are, though, various points at which you need to sign things off or ask for a re-working:

- Storyboard: when the initial ideas are drafted, with suggestions about interviewees and schedules.
- Script: a script is usually developed before the interviews and other material are recorded. This is refined once the material has been gathered. Checks and changes can be made at both stages.
- Rough edit: first the producer makes a note on paper of the different material to be used and the order. Then during a rough edit the interviews and other elements are sewn together. The elements can be shuffled and new ingredients added fairly easily.
- Final edit stages: at this point the material is refined, the sound levels are all adjusted, music and other effects are added.

When you first hear the tape – when it is loosely edited together – you might think it sounds very baggy. However, once you have agreed in principle that the right noises and words are in the right places all the extraneous sounds and pauses will be removed, music will be put in place and the whole thing should sound tight and professional.

The content

The content of a tailor-made cassette will usually sound quite similar to a radio programme. You can record interviews with people in a variety of locations. There will be some interviews recorded in soundproof studios, others will be recorded in natural surroundings with background 'atmos' noise (this is the natural noise you would expect to hear in the location). You might include the voice of the interviewer/commentator, or people might speak for themselves.

You can use documentary, drama, humour, pacey music-backed soundbites or mock news reports. The approach should be appropriate to your audience and, importantly, reflect the values and style of your organisation.

An audio tape can be longer than a video. You can break it up into 15 or 30 minute segments. People are familiar with the idea of dipping in and out of audio tapes. You might even add your own adverts or stings to break it up.

CASE STUDY
....
The Centre for Studies on Inclusive Education (CSIE) produces a variety of materials, including an audio tape pack and guidebook on how to respond to a diversity of children with disabilities or learning difficulties. The CSIE has used audio tape so that it could present six documentary 'slices of life'. Individual children in six English schools could express their own views and experiences. The accompanying print draws out particular themes and discussion points.
....

Packaging
....
The packaging you use for your audio cassettes will probably depend on which type they are – talking books or tailor-made.

The talking book materials will need a label on the body of the cassette – usually provided when they are duplicated, but you can run them off through an office laser-printer. They can then be placed in clear plastic cases. You will be able to see the label through the case. You might also bundle the cassettes up and store them in a clearly marked box to make things easier.

Tailor-made audio cassettes need glossier packaging. The company duplicating the tapes will usually provide labels with your agreed wording. They often offer to print cassette inlay cards or jackets too. You might prefer to work through your designer to get this done.

CHAPTER SIX

Video

Video is another way in which you can promote your organisation, services and particular message. It is relatively expensive to produce a broadcast-quality video, so you will probably only produce one or two every few years. Given the cost involved it's worth investing quite a bit of your own time in selecting the right company to work with and in supporting them as they produce the video.

If you want to video a piece of project work so that you have a visual record to show to other members of the team then you might just capture it on camcorder. If, however, you are using video to help with fundraising, volunteer recruitment and other promotional work then you will probably find it more valuable to have a professionally produced and edited tape.

The different uses of video

Video can be used in various ways with different audiences, to help with your promotional work. Different types of video include:

- Information films – about your organisation, its work, its people, specific projects . . . these might be used with clients, volunteers, staff, supporters and other interested parties.
- Direct fundraising appeals – with examples of how contributions are used. Such films would be sent to appropriate existing and potential donors.

- Educational programmes – to be used within the school curriculum, raising awareness of your work and relevant issues. You should make the programme to suit the age group that you are targeting. And you should remember the different curricula that apply in different parts of the UK. Production companies specialising in educational videos are listed in the *IVCA Handbook*.

- Presentations about your work – to be used at conferences, exhibitions etc. The audience for such a video could be very diverse, so the programme would need to be simple, direct and clear.

You can adapt the way in which you use the video, and you can have different versions produced in the editing process. You need to decide on this before shooting so that you have sufficient relevant material, and you certainly need to be clear, before the editing stage, about how many versions you want because it will cost you more money to ask for it to be re-edited.

Once you have a video you might want to use it in other ways. You might send out copies in answer to student enquiries about your work. You might make it available to journalists who want to use footage to illustrate a particular news story.

These other uses follow on from the main purpose. When you are producing the video it's important to focus on the main use otherwise you can end up with a video which tries to speak to everyone and satisfies no-one.

Consider your audience

CASE STUDY

Dave Dunn, Marketing Manager at Leonard Cheshire says; 'The first stage should always be to think about your intended audience – is it for the general public; potential service users; or professional decision making bodies? Effective promotion to each of these audiences depends on a highly focused approach.

'The length of the film is also important and again depends on your target audience. For some audiences you can probably

cover everything in five minutes; for others you might need two
or three times as long to get over a more rounded view of your
organisation.'
· · · · · · · · ·

However you intend to use your video it's worth remembering
the strengths and weaknesses of the medium. Video is great at
generating 'heat not light'. Video stirs the emotions, it can
motivate and illustrate. But it isn't good at imparting a lot of
information. That's why video is often accompanied by printed
material – explaining things further or reminding you of
particular points.

Most videos can hold their audience comfortably for 10 to 15
minutes. Beyond that the audience will get fidgety unless the
content is absolutely compelling or continually surprising.

Working out your approach
· · · · · · · · ·

When you have decided that you need a video for a specific
purpose you still won't know exactly what it will look like. The
particular use and audience won't automatically define the look
and feel.

To help you work out the sort of approach you might want to go
for we have listed some of the options below. You can mix and
match the following elements as appropriate:

- Pieces to camera/talking heads – interviewees speak directly
  to camera. They might be filmed in their natural location
  (from building site to office), against a plain/coloured
  backdrop, or be superimposed over a moving image (perhaps
  in slow motion).

- In-vision presenter/interviewer – someone appears on
  camera and guides you through the video. The presenter
  might be a celebrity or they might be an unknown
  professional.

- Voice-over – the presenter is never seen on-screen. A voice
  guides you through the video.

- Documentary – the audience follows people in their everyday lives. At one end of the spectrum this approach is 'fly-on-the-wall' with snatches of natural conversation, at the other extreme it is a series of quite stage-managed images.

- Interviews – these can be conducted with an in-vision presenter or with an off-camera interviewer. The interviewee might speak directly to the camera or be looking off to the side towards the interviewer.

- Collages – a sequence of stunning, unusual and intriguing pictures can be used to tell a story or convey a particular feeling.

- Drama – good quality drama is expensive to produce, but you might make use of short bursts of drama to illustrate a wider video. You will need an experienced writer, professional actors, rehearsal time, costumes etc. to ensure the drama looks good and is pitched at the right level for the audience. The production company should find you writers and actors. If you need to approach any directly *The White Book* is very useful and details are given in Further Help.

- Animation – cartoon animation can be very expensive. A few animated line-drawing characters might be appropriate. A Disney-number would be out of the question. There are a few specialist animation companies listed in the *IVCA Handbook* and Kemps' *UK Film, TV and Video Handbook*. Many animators are freelance and would work through the video production company you commission.

- Graphics and video effects – the quality of graphics and video effects has improved dramatically over recent years. You can hope for more than a page turn and flying logo. There are sophisticated and subtle graphics and mixes between images. You should discuss these elements at the briefing stage as they will affect costs.

- Music – you can use library music or commission an original score. It's often economical in the long term to commission a new piece of music which you own the rights to, however the video is shown. Kemps' *UK Film, TV and Video Handbook* and

The White Book have useful contact details. However, the
video production company should organise music on
your behalf.

Rights and release forms

If you are using actors, music and presenters then you need to
state clearly how the video will be used – in private homes,
screenings to large audiences, broadcast, in the UK, overseas
etc. And you need them to agree to this use in their contracts.
This is very important as, if you don't, you might have to pay
extra later to buy the rights to use the video in this way.

Similarly, any interviewees/participants should sign release
forms. These forms say that the participants are happy for you
to edit their interview and for the video to be used in a variety
of ways.

The video company should provide these forms and be
responsible for their completion.

Accessibility

When you are planning your video you need to decide on
whether it will be accessible to all of your intended audience.

Do you, for instance, need to produce a Welsh-language
version? Are there other languages you need to consider? If you
are providing a different language voice-over then usually two
versions of the film are made available back-to-back on the same
tape – one in the English language and one in the other
language.

You also need to consider whether to provide sub-titles. There
are several specialist firms offering this service and your video
company will advise you and make necessary arrangements.

Also, should you provide a signed version?

If you are going to sign and/or sub-title the video then the
production company needs to know this before they begin.

When they are filming they will bear this in mind. When they are deciding on an appropriate shot they will consider how it will look with the inclusion of a signer and sub-titles.

Commissioning and control

Commissioning a video production is similar to commissioning an audio tape.

It is usual to invite at least three, possibly more, video companies to pitch for the work. You might want to meet them, describe the project to all three at once and invite questions before asking them to write up their ideas and eligibility.

When inviting companies to tender you need to give them a clear brief to pitch against otherwise you won't be able to compare like with like.

The brief should be clear about:

- the main contents, flavour and messages;
- the target audience and principal use;
- the expected length of the video (usually 10–15 minutes);
- the production values you expect (broadcast quality or something less than this);
- the number of different locations involved (each will probably need one day of filming);
- any stylistic guidelines you think are appropriate (eg 'we don't want something that looks like a traditional corporate video of interviews with the "suits"; we want something that looks natural – more like a fly on the wall than PR', etc.);
- a ballpark budget figure – a 10–15 minute documentary/information video produced to broadcast quality would usually cost around £25,000;
- other possible elements such as supporting print, the need for duplication etc.

The process

It is worth knowing the different stages involved in producing
a video. This will help you to retain the right degree of control,
and to plan effectively.

Outline brief

The first stage is to come up with an outline brief. This is issued
to companies who are invited to tender for the production.
When they submit their proposals they will usually make some
creative suggestions. However, it is after the selection process
that you will really start to firm things up.

You will have a meeting to discuss your brief in further detail.
This meeting is partly about clarifying ideas and partly to
establish working relationships. Some of the important things to
agree at this stage are:

- a production timetable;
- key contacts and overall project manager on both sides;
- target filming dates and locations;
- essential messages to incorporate;
- number of copies required;
- checking procedure/sign-off points;
- the budget and procedures for keeping to costs.

Research and development

The next phase is research and development. Research will
cover the people to be featured, the locations in which they will
appear and any props/materials that need to be incorporated.
The production company will want to meet people to consider
how they will come across on screen. They will also want to see
the settings in which these people will be filmed.

Research is all about checking things out and coming up with
options. So, it might be that the production company will visit
some people and projects that don't eventually make it onto the
screen. It's important that people are clear about this so that
they are not disappointed if they aren't filmed.

The production company will come up with a draft script/storyboard. Usually this is a written description of the images that will be used alongside any likely interview comments and voice-over. If appropriate some of the images or graphics might be drawn and mounted onto A3.

This will give you an idea of the shape and general content. The producer will work to this script when they film. Whilst the script indicates the sort of thing someone might say when interviewed, it isn't a word-for-word reference.

Usually you will have the opportunity to look at the draft script, make comments and amendments and sign it off before filming begins. Don't just look at what is included in it, also look at what might be missed out. You can add items at this stage; it's easier to cut things out after they've been filmed than to create them afterwards.

The schedule

The production company will draw up a schedule for the shoot. You can attend some, all or none of the filming days – it's up to you. The schedule will include maps, contact numbers and timings.

Paper edit

After the filming the production company will do what's known as a 'paper edit'. They look at the rushes (the video tapes and transcripts from the filming) and they note the various shots and words they want to use in approximately the right order. You might want to have a meeting to discuss this so that you can advise them of any sensitivities in what they have selected or query anything that has been left out.

Off-line and on-line edits

Next, the production company will do an off-line or rough edit. They actually assemble all the shots in the order in which they will appear. They include interviews and put on a guide voice track – giving the words a voice-over will contain, but not going to the expense of hiring a presenter at this stage.

It helps if the production company presents the off-line to you, giving you details of how things might be mixed together, where music might be used and generally explaining why it looks so rough. If the rough is just sent to people without the appropriate context, they can get the wrong idea of how the finished version will look.

If there are corrections to be made at this stage it is still possible and not too expensive to make them. Usually a production company will be ready to do half a day of minor editing repairs to the rough. Then they go into the on-line and dub. Here all of the subtle finishing touches are made. The sound is levelled out and music and voice-over are added. Graphics are also added at this stage. It is very expensive to make changes after the on-line is finished, so you need to sign off the off-line with confidence.

You might want to drop in at the on-line edit stage, to reassure yourself that everything is going as you hoped. Check any captions giving people's job titles and ensure that names and titles are pronounced correctly in the voice-over.

Once you have signed off this finished on-line video you will have a master tape. Usually you will duplicate copies from a sub-master. This gives you a safety net in case anything happens to your expensive original.

Being filmed

Who should appear in your video? Some people will, of course, be desperate to be on camera. Others will be camera-shy. Unfortunately the keen ones aren't always the appropriate ones. And the appropriate ones aren't always articulate on-screen.

Sometimes you will want to feature a manager. At other times a volunteer or client will be the most appropriate spokesperson.

The good news is that most videos are filmed by crews of just three people – a director/producer, camera person and sound/lighting person. By the time they have set up all their equipment and run through how things will work you could feel like old friends. This all helps to make the atmosphere relaxed and informal. And remember that if you are paying the bills, you aren't going to get a grilling by an aggressive reporter.

You are all part of the same team and they will be trying to help you look good and say the right thing. If you make a mistake you can do it again. If you aren't happy with what you have said you can ask to do it again. Rarely will you see huge chunks of speech in a video. So the producer can use snippets in various places, removing the bad bits, using your voice with different pictures (visuals).

You might have to repeat the same thing a number of times for other reasons. The director might want to see you from different angles, or up close and from further away. There might be problems with the sound or lights that mean you need to have another go. The camera might not be up and running when you launch into your answer. A plane might fly overhead. A cow might moo... In fact, a great deal of patience is needed because filming takes a long time.

Branding

The whole video is a promotion for your organisation and your work. So, many people will be mentioning the charity's name as they talk about what they do or how they have benefited. You don't have to rely solely on what people say. You can reinforce your branding in other ways.

You might, for instance, have some people wearing T-shirts or sweatshirts with your logo on. This would be most appropriate if you are showing staff or volunteers at work. It would be less appropriate if your chief executive is being interviewed in their office. The chief executive could, though, have some sort of logo behind or beside them – anything from an exhibition panel to a branded paperweight.

You can go for a more subtle approach involving use of the corporate colours and typefaces within the video. Graphics saying who people are or presenting information visually might make use of particular fonts and colours. You might include people filmed against particular colours or wearing your organisation's colours.

Many organisations like to kick off their video with a message from a senior manager or their patron. This has started to look a bit old-fashioned. It's not a technique which is used in television programmes, so it feels very 'corporate video'. It might be better to have this important person talking about the organisation in an informal environment at a later point in the video, fitting in naturally but giving a weighty endorsement at the same time.

Packaging

Finally in this section of video production, we are going to look at packaging.

As the video is being duplicated a label will be stuck on each copy. You can commission such labels through your designer or you can tell the video duplicator what information you want to include and they will produce the labels for you. The information might be the name of the production company, the video title, any copyright statement and possibly the running time.

The copyright statement usually says © your charity's name and charity number, with the date. You might want to add your own reference number.

You will also need to produce a cassette jacket – usually you will commission a designer to develop this, but you might ask the video duplicator to create one. You might go for a sheet which is slightly smaller than A4 – when folded this becomes front, back and spine and it is tucked into the front of the video case. There are also cases with separate holes for covers, spines and backs. Most duplicators have a variety of cases on offer, so it's up to you to choose which you prefer.

The sort of things to print on a video jacket include:

- a picture or illustration which captures the spirit of the video and gives a clear idea of the type of content;
- the title and details of who is issuing the video (ie your organisation);
- your logo in a prominent position;
- details of any price charged for the video;
- a brief description of the contents and target audience;
- the length of the video;
- any sponsors;
- contact details for further information/copies.

You can pick up on any corporate colours on the jacket and follow logo positioning guidelines.

If the video is being made available with supporting print then you might want a package which binds the two together. The usual way of doing this is to provide the duplicated videos, labelled and in cases, to the printer who is producing the rest of the material. It's quite a complicated timetable, but essentially the following would happen:

- designer develops theme for all materials and lays materials out;
- designer prepares video jacket (and labels);
- video jacket and labels are printed and supplied to video duplicator;
- remaining material is designed and printed;
- duplicated videos, labelled and in cases, are supplied to printers;
- printer binds all print and video together in one package.

This sort of packaging might, however, seem wasteful and you may decide against it on environmental as well as cost grounds.

CHAPTER SEVEN

Using a Website

The Internet provides another way of getting your message across and raising your profile.

You might simply set yourself up with an e-mail address which enables you to send and receive messages electronically. A list of free e-mail providers can be found on CharityNet at www.charitynet.org   More and more, however, charities and other organisations are choosing to put information about themselves on a Website.

Most people come into contact with the World Wide Web by surfing in on their personal computer. With a modem or ISDN line, an Internet service provider and the right software on your computer you can just dial in and search for the information you are after. The Web is like a vast library at your fingertips. But in reality it doesn't physically exist in one place. A network of server computers store different bits of the information. Your organisation's details can be stored on one of these computers. But as we'll see in the section on 'location and links' your information can apparently be in many different places at once.

Opportunities

The Web has been around for a while, but it is developing and expanding all the time. But the fact that it is a growing medium isn't a good enough reason to hop aboard. So, why might a charity want to have some sort of presence on the Web?

- To inform and raise your profile – people use the Web as a giant database. They might be doing research as students, they might be journalists developing an article, they might be potential clients who need details of your services, anyone who has an interest in subjects covered on your site.

- To fundraise – there are a variety of ways in which people fundraise on the Web – through on-line auctions, products that are for sale, appeals and sponsorship details.

- To conduct research – you might have an on-line questionnaire to gather information about the people who are interested in your work, who surf into your Website.

- To promote specific services – for instance, you might want to promote a list of forthcoming events, a helpline service, or details of support literature.

Gradual development

The great thing about a Website is that it can change and grow over time. It's not like producing a video where a big investment results in a single product that gradually dates and eventually needs to be completely replaced. Here are some of the options:

Electronic directory entry

Your first venture onto the Web might be to be listed in another organisation's directory. Your contact details and a brief description of your work might be all that appears. You could have an e-mail address which people can click onto and immediately send you a message. It is unlikely that you will be listed without someone first contacting you to check that your details are correct, even if they are ringing you to confirm your entry in the paper-based version. You can ask to be included in some of these on-line directories, but you need to do some research first to find out where it would be appropriate to appear. Most such directories will list you free of charge.

Electronic 'promotional flier'

You might go a step further and have a single page, which is a
bit like an electronic version of an advert or flier. There are a
number of organisations offering charities a free page or even
a free set of pages. They might provide you with a template
which you just fill in, perhaps with your logo to make it more
personalised. There is a list of some of the organisations offering
free or low cost space at www.contact.orgs/frspace.htm   It is
also worth looking at CharityNet non-profit pages and
www.garrick.co.uk/charity.html and www.vois.org.uk for more
information.

Electronic 'brochure'

The third option is to have a full-blown Website, which is like an
electronic brochure. You can include several pages, pictures,
and information on a variety of relevant topics. We outline this
in more detail in the section on content below.

You might gradually expand your Web presence until you reach
this stage or you might decide to go for a site straight away. Even
when you have a site it will be constantly developing (see the
section on Updating).

Developing a Website

Once you've decided that you want a Website, how do you go
about getting one up and running?

The first two things you need to decide are:

- What do you want the site to achieve?
- How big do you want the site to be (how much do you want
  to include)?

If the site is purely to sell the products offered by your charity's
trading arm, then it will look very different to a site designed to
disseminate the latest medical research.

If you want to include on-line versions of all your leaflets then it
will look different to a site that includes headlines and tasters

which prompt people to get in touch and order booklets. Such tasters might include introductions and summaries of the booklets or comments from reviewers.

When you have an idea of the main content you hope to include you might want to find an agency to design and programme the material for your site. You can work through an organisation that will also host your site (giving it an address, making it available 24 hours a day and feeding you any responses). You might use an independent Web design agency, listed in *Yellow Pages* or in the *Multimedia Yearbook* (see Further Help).

As with other production work, you will need to brief these agencies and work together to come up with a workable design featuring your branding.

Most Web design agencies will give you an address on the Web where you can see the work-in-progress, comment on it and see how things appear on screen.

The alternative is to design and programme the site yourself. That's what Contact a Family did, as assistant director Dean Casswell explains:

CASE STUDY
· · · · · · · · ·
'It wasn't nearly as complicated as I thought it would be. I am quite computer literate, but I was surprised at how relatively easy it is to put things on the Web. At first I began reading a book about programming material in HTML – the computer language used on the Internet. I started to learn all the codes. Then I found some software that converts it all for you anyway.'
· · · · · · · · ·

Attracting people to your site
· · · · · · · · ·
What are the most important factors to consider in setting up your Website? Some people might say 'location, location, location' but actually 'location, links, search engines, and promotions' would be more appropriate.

There is no point in being on the Web unless people visit your site. How do you attract them?

- by your positioning;
- by pulling people in from other sites via 'hotlinks';
- by having interesting words on your site that people might search for.

Location

You might find it appropriate to be positioned in a general area amongst other charities or NGOs. If you are in a general area of this kind then people who already have an interest in the work of charities will find it easier to track you down. Also if someone is looking at a site covering a related issue they are more likely to visit your site, because they will see your listing in the area's overview/guide.

Another factor is credibility. If you are located within a well-regarded charity Website then you benefit from the goodwill associated with the site.

There are various charity supersites on the Web such as CharityNet and OneWorldOnline (for developmental charities). You just need to get in contact with the relevant project co-ordinators to find out how much this might cost and how you go about supplying them with the materials they need. The project co-ordinator's details will appear on their site and usually include e-mail and telephone contact numbers.

Links

Another way of ensuring people visit your site is through a series of hotlinks. These are virtual pathways that allow surfers to leap from one Website to another at the click of a button. You can develop such links over time. Sometimes you will think of an appropriate link and initiate it. On other occasions someone will approach you and ask if it's OK to set up a link.

Links are helpful from the user's point of view as they save them research time, prompting them to look at related issues. They are helpful from the organisation's point of view because they attract people who already have a relevant interest to their site.

The Charities Aid Foundation site CharityNet has links to a wide range of charity sites, as well as links to grantmakers and other relevant organisations. The site is at www.charitynet.org/

Search engines

The main way in which someone will be attracted to your site is through one of several search engines. The user keys in relevant words or phrases. The search engine then does a rapid hunt and comes up with sites, pages and titles which more or less match the words or phrases given in the search request. The results are offered up according to how well they match the search words – 100 per cent or less.

Someone who finds your site by this method will already be actively trying to discover more. Their interest may be narrow, but you already have someone who is receptive to your message.

To ensure search engines find and refer people to your site, you will need to include relevant words and phrases – using them frequently to increase your position in the search engine's listing.

You can test this out by doing 'mystery shopper' tests with the different search engines to see whether or not they list your site.

Other promotions

Another way of attracting people to your site is through written and other promotions. You might print your Web address on your letterhead, brochures or a promotional flier/postcard, etc. When you design your site you will have an opportunity to choose a name that more or less reflects your charity name. But you need to promote the actual address as you would if you moved buildings. You might include details on your fax header urging people to visit your site. You could sign off your e-mails with a message about your Web pages.

Keeping people at your site

It's one thing attracting people to your site, it's another matter to keep them there.

If someone finds your site by using a search engine, then you can programme your site so that it remains in a window when the user clicks out of their search.

That's a simple technical procedure. More important, though, is to ensure that you have a site that loads quickly (so the user doesn't get bored and abandon their browsing). And you want a site that is interesting and full of different elements that the user might want to dip into.

Do you want them to return? You might include details of how regularly your site is updated. You might invite them to join an on-line forum or news group so that you can keep them posted on matters of interest.

Structure and design

Most Website structures, when drawn out on paper, look like a family tree.

You start off with a home page. This branches out into four or five second tier pages. Then each of these branches out into up to four or five more and so on.

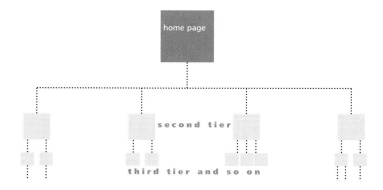

Figure 12

You can develop further layers within each sub-section.

At every layer you will have an on-screen button that returns you to the home page. You might also have buttons relating to the second tier too.

The important thing to remember is how someone visiting the site for the first time would find their way around. You have to make it as easy as possible to 'navigate'.

You also need to make the site easy to load and look at – this is all about the design. Pictures look good and make the page brighter, but too many mean the page takes a long time to load. People can be put off by a long wait, so it's important to strike a balance between impact and loading time.

And if pictures seem to take a time to load, video clips, sound and animations take even longer. If you are going to use any of these devices it might be better to use them at a lower tier. That way they are already involved in the site and probably more prepared to wait a bit.

Another point to remember on the design side is that colour and appearance can vary depending on the type of computer and software people use to go on the Web. Try to view your site from different machines to give yourself a fair picture.

Content

Just what material should go onto a Website? Opinions vary and that's why the World Wide Web is so diverse and interesting. Some organisations and individuals publish thousands of words on their sites. Others offer people the chance to exchange views on a particular issue. Some ask you to give your details before you can look at their site, others give you the chance to contact them if they want more information.

Have a look at other people's sites before deciding what to include in your own.

· · · · · · · · ·

Dean Casswell of Contact a Family did this sort of research when he was designing the charity's site at www.cafamily.org.uk.

'If you look at what other people have done with their Websites it helps you to get an idea of what works, what you like and what you will want to try to mimic,' says Dean.

'You will quickly realise that tons of graphics take ages to download, so the person browsing will get fed up and go away. If you put too much on the page they'll be forever scrolling through the information.'

Contact a Family has two main strands to its Website. One of these is general information about the charity, with leaflets, edited articles from its quarterly newsletter, regional contacts etc. The other main strand is a pay-per-view section. This is an on-line version of its directory of conditions and disabilities affecting children.

The paper version of the directory raises eight per cent of the charity's income. So it didn't want to lose this income stream by making the directory freely available on the Web. At the same time, though, Contact a Family wanted to support parents who would have a very specific interest in one or two entries in the directory.

The charity came up with an elegant solution making use of available technology: the medical profession and others using the directory regularly have to pay for access. However, others can use a guest account to access the directory up to three times for free.
· · · · · · · · ·

Below we give some ideas about what you might want to include in your site.

Background/wallpaper You can make use of your logo and identity in a subtle embossed background to all your pages.

A home page This will have a very general message and the organisation's logo. Mainly it is about signposting the rest of the site. It's a bit like a contents page or menu. You can include simple animated symbols which rotate or flash.

Further menus These might be included in the second tier. They act as contents pages for the various sub-sections.

Site search engines These are common on larger Websites. They allow people to search through your site using key words or phrases.

Services and projects Often publicised on Websites. You can tell people what is going on, attract their interest and involvement, and share good practice.

Research documents and leaflets Such material can be reproduced on Websites. This enables people to go into your site and extract relevant information in their own time. It saves you the cost of postage and answering queries over the phone.

Events Can be listed in diary form – it's important to keep such information as up to date as possible.

News You might reproduce news releases and newsletters or you might re-write information in a shorter form to make it easier to read on-screen.

Frequently asked questions The answers to these are usually included as they raise common queries and/or myths. You can give a detailed reply and refer people to other relevant sites for further information. This can be a useful resource for researchers.

Questionnaires A good way of gathering information on who is using your Website. People can visit most sites anonymously so you might want to make a questionnaire optional. Alternatively you might offer them the chance to fill in some of the information whilst not saying who they are. It all depends on why you want the information and how you intend to use it. You might want to build up a mailing list (in which case you do need all their details). But you might just want help in evaluating and improving your site (in which case anonymous replies would be fine). In designing such questionnaires bear in mind the sensitivity of any information you gather, and ensure you comply with the Data Protection Act (see Further Help).

You can have a questionnaire which appears before someone enters your site. Or you can have a questionnaire attached to a specific area within the site.

Reply forms These appear on most sites. They allow users to fill in their details along with an enquiry, or to get in touch with a personal message. Usually there is an e-mail response, but phone and written address details also appear.

Competitions and quizzes They prompt users to send through their details and they give a sense of involvement and fun.

Fora/information exchanges Allow users either to chat in real time or to post their ideas and messages to one another. This can be a good way of finding out people's views. You can also invite people to 'subscribe' to an e-mail update list.

Merchandise You can sell your merchandise over the Web. You can use various devices to keep people's credit details secure. Your Website can act like an electronic catalogue which people view at their convenience. Your Web design agency will be able to advise you on the different options for secure transactions. They can set up sites so that users browse through and click on the different items they want to put in their electronic shopping basket. When the user is ready the cost of their shopping is added up. They pay by credit card over the Web and you dispatch their goods once your bank has cleared their payment.

Fundraising forms You can reproduce your forms on-line. You might provide information on making legacies, you might give details of on-line sponsorship opportunities. You could use the CharityNet free flag page 'Ways of Giving'.

Adverts These can be included in your site. It's one of the ways you might raise the money to produce and update your Web pages. It's just like selling sponsorship and advertising on printed material. You will need to set a ratecard and approach potential advertisers. Perhaps it can be an add-on option if you sell adverts in your newsletter – for a small additional fee the advertiser can appear on your Website as well as in your newsletter.

Branding
· · · · · · · · ·

Your Website should be easily identifiable as *yours*. It should
follow through on your corporate identity – using the same
logo and style guidelines; picking up on key colours; using
appropriate wording; and perhaps using a distinctive
background/wallpaper.

This is easier for smaller single-site organisations to achieve
than those with many departments or branches.

CASE STUDY
· · · · · · · · ·

Nigel Tuckett from Scope says: 'New projects arise and naturally
want to promote themselves on the Web. They often want their
own separate site, and they're not always clear on the need to
follow the overall corporate identity. Further, we don't want
someone who is surfing through a search engine to be confused
if they find lots of different Scope sites.'
· · · · · · · · ·

Updating
· · · · · · · · ·

When you set up a Website you need to establish a system for
updating it. This should include a regular review, additions and
deletions. Unfortunately, many individuals and organisations
have a burst of enthusiasm for the Web, invest a bit of time,
energy and money into a site and then forget about it.

Old news can be left on the Website for useful background. This
needs to be listed in an appropriate way so that users are clear it
hasn't just been overlooked. Old diary dates should be removed
as soon as they are passed.

CASE STUDY
· · · · · · · · ·

Contact a Family has built in a Web dimension to all of its
publications work. If a factsheet needs to be amended, then the
Website is also changed at the same time. There are regular
monthly updates to the site. And the charity also uses a
programme to test out all its external links to ensure they are
up-to-date.

'There's always more that can be done to a Website. You can never feel that it is finished. You can always add something', says Dean Casswell.

·········

Feedback
·········

Feedback of some kind should be built into your Web design, otherwise you might never know if it has been worth doing. Usage statistics are normally available. But 300 'hits' from people in America might mean little to a small charity with a very local remit. Most feedback forms allow people to e-mail you directly from your Website with their enquiry.

Credibility
·········

The beauty of the Web is that almost anyone can put information on it. However, this can also be considered a downside. Users might ask themselves just how reliable the information is if it can go onto the Web unchecked.

There are various ways to address this, including giving clear sources and references for any information you put onto your site. You can also ask external bodies to look at your site and give it a rating or award.

Accessibility
·········

Another important consideration is how accessible your Website is to people with a visual impairment, learning disability or first language other than English.

Visual impairment
··········

You might want to include details of how to increase the point size of the text used on your site. You might take readability into consideration when you are designing the layout of each page. In addition, you might include some information on audio, so that at a click of a button the user can download spoken details.

Learning disabilities

You might have a section of the Website which makes use of symbols and pictures, so that it is accessible to people with learning disabilities. Making this section fairly interactive will help.

First language other than English

You might want to include information in other languages. You can reproduce your entire Website in different languages with a choice on your Home Page. Your Web design agency should be able to help you to set this in place.

CHAPTER EIGHT

Using CD-ROM

CD-ROM is another medium you might use to promote your charity. It allows the user to dip in and out of information in much the same way as the World Wide Web. You can generally move around a CD-ROM at greater speed because you look at it off-line. And you will probably include more information on the CD-ROM than on a Website.

We look at some of the ways in which you might use CD-ROM below, before talking about how you get one produced, plus some of the branding issues.

Appropriate uses

There are various materials that you might produce on CD-ROM. Often you will mirror a piece of print. Sometimes CD-ROM will be the only format you use.

Directories/Databases work well on CD-ROM. If you produce a directory which people search through, then they might prefer an electronic version. If you do this, then consider how a third party might make use of the information, particularly if there is any sensitivity around data protection (see Further Help).

Educational materials can be made available on CD-ROM. However, publishers are increasingly using the World Wide Web as this makes distribution easier and schools can get access at little or no cost.

Forms and templates, in fact any material that you might produce for people on disc, can be produced on CD-ROM with its greater storage space. You might make materials available to people outside your organisation – sharing good practice. Equally, you might use CD-ROM to ensure everyone in your charity is using the same format and branding. Scope, for instance, is considering CD as a vehicle for its corporate identity. Templates and guidelines would be available on CD-ROM. Different branches would be able to work from the discs when developing their own materials.

Production

So, how do you go about producing a CD-ROM? It's similar to the production of audio, video and Web materials. You work with a production company – inviting several to bid before commissioning your selected agency. *The White Book*, Kemps' *UK film, TV and Video Handbook* and *The Multimedia Yearbook* all list details of CD-ROM production companies. Details are in Further Help.

The content of your CD-ROM will dictate the amount of work involved in its production (and therefore the price). If you are reproducing some standard forms and templates that have already been created on computer then there is little more to do except burn the data into the CD.

A little conversion work might be needed in producing a CD-ROM version of a database/directory. However, if you are producing some educational materials, or developing a CD-ROM game then there is a lot of development, design and testing to be done – the cost will reflect this.

The duplication of CD-ROMs is straightforward and relatively cheap – around a £1 a copy.

Branding
....

There are two key areas of branding to consider if you are
producing a CD-ROM for use outside your charity.

The first is the on-screen appearance. The second is the labelling
and packaging of the CD-ROM.

The on-screen branding is important because:

- CDs often get separated from their covers;
- people will spend more time looking at the screen of their
  computer than at the packaging;
- if people print out information they have grabbed off the
  screen it is important that you have a credit/branding if the
  information changes hands.

Branding on-screen can come in various places. You can have
an upfront credit with your logo and message as people open the
CD-ROM. You can have a credit and contact details at the end
(as people go through a procedure to quit or exit). Within the
CD-ROM you might have a logo or message on a bar at the side
or at the head/foot of each page. Or you might have a credit at
key points within the CD-ROM.

The label of the CD-ROM should have the title and your charity
name together with any other information you feel to be
relevant. The case should have a single sheet or small booklet
with further information and contact details.

CHAPTER NINE

Merchandise

In this chapter we look at promotional merchandise. Such merchandise can range from 'freebies' that are given away at exhibitions through to products that people pay for. The thing that they have in common is that they all carry your branding and messages. Whether people pay for them or not, they all help to promote your organisation to a wider audience.

Different types of and uses for merchandise

Let's look in more detail now at some of the different types of merchandise and the various ways they can be used.

Different types of merchandise

There are two main types of merchandise. These are:

- freebie give-aways;
- paid-for products.

The freebie give-aways will be for low cost items that are produced in bulk. The sort of goods that might be given away at little or no cost include:

- pens and pencils;
- balloons;
- bags;
- stickers;
- badges.

The paid-for products will be for higher-value goods, probably produced in smaller numbers. They include the following type of item:

- mugs;
- T-shirts;
- sweat shirts;
- umbrellas;
- diaries and calendars;
- baseball hats.

Different uses for merchandise

Merchandise can be used for various purposes. If you are giving things away at an exhibition it can help to attract people to your stand. Once you have their attention you can then tell them more about your organisation and your work. Once they have left the event then the merchandise acts in a different way; it helps them to remember you. So items which have a degree of durability are most appropriate.

Paid-for items are more likely to be bought by someone who is already in touch or involved with the organisation. These items are about:

- bringing in additional income;
- advertising your organisation (people wearing your shirts act as walking billboards);
- keeping your organisation in the minds of your supporters.

Promoting your merchandise

Freebies need little promotion – in fact they are generally an incentive to get someone to do something else: to visit an exhibition stand; to enter a competition; to return a questionnaire; to buy a product. A good display and the mere mention of their availability should be sufficient.

The paid-for items need to be actively promoted. You might:

- display some of the items on an exhibition stand (although you will need to tighten up your security if you do this);

- produce a catalogue of products/order form which is sent to all supporters, volunteers etc. (everyone on your newsletter mailing list);

- have a display of the items at your office/s, so that anyone who visits can see what is available;

- have an on-line catalogue (on your Website);

- provide products to relevant businesses or shops and supportive organisations;

- promote the items at open days and other special events when those attending are all confirmed supporters of your organisation.

Artwork and guidelines

Often organisations will quickly develop some balloons or pens for an event. Then no more merchandise is produced until an exhibition comes along. Then they will rush to produce some mugs, perhaps. The exhibition ends and all thoughts of merchandise die away too.

This is fine and means that you will probably have a specific project budget to spend against. But it also means that you won't get the cheapest deals because you are producing goods in small numbers. You might also find that items lack consistency because they are produced by different manufacturers to different people's instructions.

You might also end up with various half empty boxes of unused items tucked away wherever they will fit. No-one has any idea how much stock you have left and some items just sit there until your logo has changed and they have to be thrown away.

This is all an argument for a more coherent approach which is overseen by a single person. This person will either be the manager in charge of promotional/marketing materials, or someone working for them. So they will be working to overall house style and guidelines. A sub-set of these guidelines needs to be developed for the production of merchandise.

The guidelines should cover:

- how to use the logo in one or more colours, and in various sizes;
- appropriate colours and patterns for products;
- any catchlines that can be used, and how they should appear;
- appropriate images and messages;
- the overall impression that should be created;
- notes on appropriate materials and environmental impacts;
- reference numbers and stock control;
- delivery and storage.

Artwork should also be available to be supplied to different printers and manufacturers on disc and on paper. This means that you retain control over how your logo is adapted.

Production and checking process
·········

Once you have some guidelines you have some level of quality control. Inevitably, though, you will be working with a wide range of designers, printers and manufacturers as different companies are geared up to make different products.

You probably won't want just to hand over your guidelines, artwork for your logo and an order for the quantity of goods. There are various checks you can put in place to ensure you get what you are hoping for.

First, as with all the other production processes, look at more than one company for each of the items you are ordering. Ask them for samples and assess their quality. You might even ask them to produce some mock-ups speculatively to give you an idea of how your branding might work in practice.

CASE STUDY

Tricia Slater is Publications Admin Assistant with the People's
Dispensary for Sick Animals. The PDSA has its own printing
department and commissions merchandise centrally for its
individual branches. Tricia says: 'We work with between 30 and
35 suppliers. It's really important to talk to different suppliers
and see samples before working with them. You can find
companies in your local *Yellow Pages*. The suppliers will send
brochures and sales reps will come round to talk through your
requirements.'

Once you have commissioned a company, brief them and issue
them with your guidelines and artwork. Then ask them for
some more mock-ups of the product. Only when you are
confident that you are going to get what you have asked for
should you give the go-ahead for production.

The production company should have its own quality control
procedures to make sure that the goods are produced to one
standard. It's worth carrying out a random check of your own
and having a contract in place that commits them to the
minimum of rejects.

Appropriate images and messages

You might decide that you want to produce a mug for your
organisation. You have your guidelines on how to use the logo,
and you have your supplier in place. But a further decision is
needed and that is what else to include. Do you include an image
or some kind or a message?

It is usually worth having some sort of extra image or message.
Printing the logo and organisation name on a mug will help to
increase recognition of your branding. But it might not give
people a better understanding of what you do. A simple
sentence summarising your vision or services can help to
improve people's knowledge of your work.

Storage and stock control

When you receive your merchandise it's worth logging it and
ensuring you have some sort of stock control procedure. When
merchandise is paid for this is slightly easier because your
accounts package will log each sale and adjust the stock level
accordingly. It's slightly more complicated if you are giving
away free items. You might run these through your accounts as
costing £0. However, many accounts packages have problems
in processing items at nil cost. In this case it might be worth
keeping a separate database which you adjust each time
materials are given away. Keeping track will help you to
appreciate when you are running low and need to re-order.

Further help and information
·········

There are a number of specialist magazines dealing with the issues covered in this booklet. These include:

AV Magazine, (£45 pa) MacLarenhouse, 19 Scarbrook Road, Croydon CR9 1QH. Tel: 0171-611 0566

Broadcast, (£90 pa) EMAP Media, 33–39 Bowling Green Lane, London EC1R 0DA. Tel: 0171-505 8014

Marketing, (£75 pa) 174 Hammersmith Road, London W6 7JP. Tel: 0171-413 4150

PR Week, (free) 174 Hammersmith Road, London W6 7JP. Tel: 0171-413 4429

The BRAD Advertiser and Agency List is a useful quarterly listing of consultancies and manufacturers. It is available on subscription from Maclean Hunter House, Chalk Lane, Cockfosters Road, Barnet EN4 0BU. Tel: 0181-441 6644.

The Hollis *UK Press and PR Annual* (£97.50) is a good source of contacts, particularly if you are looking for companies which produce merchandise. It is published by **Hollis Directories Ltd**, Harlequin House, 7 High Street, Teddington TW11 8EL. Tel: 0181-977 7711.

The **IVCA** produces a *Visual Communications Handbook* (£35) which lists independent video, audio and multimedia production companies. The **International Visual Communication Association** is based at Bolsover House, 5/6 Clipstone Street, London W1P 8LD. Tel: 0171-580 0962.

The PACT *Directory of Independent Producers* (£25) lists over 400 film and independent video and television production companies. It is available from the **Producers Alliance for Cinema and Television**, 45 Mortimer Street, London S1N 7TP. Tel: 0171-331 6000.

The Creative Handbook covers design, illustration, audio and visual services. It is published by **Variety Media Publications**, 34/35 Newman Street, London W1P 3PD. Tel: 0171-637 3663.

Kemps' *UK Film, TV and Video Handbook (£41)* covers audio visual production companies and facilities. Kemps' *International Film, TV and Video Handbook* (£86) covers these services, but has an international remit. They are published by **Variety Media Publications**, 34/35 Newman Street, London W1P 3PD. Tel: 0171-637 3663.

The Multimedia Yearbook (£149 for print; £229 for CD-ROM) is a relatively expensive publication which covers CD-ROM and multimedia production. Published by **TFPL Multimedia** it is available from Macmillan, 25 Eccleston Place, London SW1W 9NF. Tel: 0171-881 8000.

The White Book (£65) contains listings of video, exhibition and entertainment production companies. It is available from Bank House, 23 Warwick Road, Coventry CV1 2EW. Tel: 01203-559658.

The Marketing and Creative Handbook is published in regional editions. It covers all aspects of advertising, marketing, exhibitions, design and publicity. The different handbooks can be viewed on the Web at www.mch.co.uk.   For more information contact Marketing and Creative Handbook, Suite 5, 74 Oak Road, Horfield, Bristol BS7 8RZ. Tel: 0117-944 6144.

Centre for Environmental Education (CEE) publishes guidelines for anyone producing environmental education resources. It is based at Reading University, London Road, Reading RG1 5AQ.

The Education Yearbook (£89) contains useful details for anyone involved in producing materials for schools. Published by **Financial Times Management** it is available from 128 Long Acre, London WC2E 9AN.

The Makaton Vocabulary Development Project is based at 31 Firwood Drive, Camberley, Surrey GU15 3QD. The project can help and advise on the production of accessible material for learning disabled readers.

The Royal National Institute for the Blind (RNIB) is based at 224 Great Portland Street, London W1N 6AA. The RNIB can advise on the production and use of Braille and large print material.

The Media Trust, 3–6 Alfred Place, London WC1E 7EB. Tel: 0171-637 4747.

The Office of the Data Protection Registrar, Wycliff House, Water Lane, Wilmslow, Cheshire SK9 5AF. Tel: 01625-545700. To find out more about the Act, contact the information line on 01625-545745.

Glossary
·········

A5, A4 and A3 paper sizes. A4 is the size of a standard piece of photocopier paper or letterhead. A3 is twice as large as A4. A5 is half as large as A4.

Artwork the finished design prepared for printing.

Brand an identity created with words and graphics that distinguishes a project or organisation from others.

By-line the author's acknowledgement. Either a simple 'by xxx' or a sentence containing that author's name.

Cassette master the top copy or original which is produced. This is kept in safe storage.

Cassette sub-master the second copy which is used for duplication and other processes. If it gets damaged, another sub-master can be produced from the original master.

Cromalin the document produced by a printer for the client to check and approve. It shows the colours to be used and is as close as possible to how the finished product will appear.

Commission giving an individual or organisations instructions to produce something for you with an agreed timetable and budget.

Copy the text written for a publication.

Copyright statement. A message on a cassette or other product informing users of the copyright holder for the product. Usually © xxx and a date.

Crop cutting out inappropriate sections from a picture in order to focus on its essential elements.

Digital printing a process which allows low-cost printing for a small print run (less than 500 copies).

Dub adjusting and adding sound.

Duotone reproduction of a photograph using two chosen colours. Duotones help to give a publication a modern feel.

Font the style of letters used; the 'typeface'.

Four colour printing a printing process mixing the colours cyan, magenta, yellow and black to form other colours and to reproduce colour photographs.

Gatefold a document is folded in two places rather than in half to give two flaps and a central panel.

Lamination a process giving a matt or gloss finish which makes print stiffer, stainproof and brighter.

Landscape a document which is short and wide in shape.

Laser printing the printing used in most offices with a computer and desktop printer.

Leading the amount of white space between lines of type.

Logo an image, name, letters or symbol, or combination of these which captures the personality of your charity and is your organisation's distinctive badge.

Masthead the distinctive name and logo for a newsletter at the top of the front page of each edition.

Mock-ups samples of products as they will look when manufactured for you to amend or approve.

Overprint using a pre-printed letterhead or leaflet and adding text and other information – usually printed through a desktop printer.

Pick list setting out options with tick boxes for the user to select (for instance, on a fax having the option of ticking an 'urgent' box).

Portrait a document which is tall and thin in shape.

Print run the number of copies produced at one time.

Proof-read reading through a document to check for and amend spelling and grammatical errors.

Ratecard the amounts of money charged for different products or services set out in a written document.

Rushes the video tapes of all the filming.

Sans serif/serif fonts can either have loops on their 'f's, 'g's etc., like handwriting (serif) or have plain ascenders and descenders (sans serif).

Scan the process by which a computer 'reads' a picture, photo or similar image and converts it into digital information which can be manipulated and printed.

Sealed a process which prevents ink rubbing off on the reader's hands.

Sign-off the formal process by which you say you are happy with something and agree it is ready to go to the next stage. Sign-offs can be verbal or in writing.

Soundbite a short punchy phrase which can be used in a variety of contexts.

Specification the detailed instructions of the work you are commissioning from an individual or organisation.

Spot colour a second colour used to highlight and enhance a piece of print.

Sting a short sequence of music or words repeated to build familiarity, convey a message and punctuate a production.

Storyboard the document submitted by a production company to show the different elements planned for their production – sound, vision etc., in the relevant order.

Strapline a slogan used with your logo to give more information about your charity's aims and work.

Style guide a document with examples and instructions on how to use an organisation's logo and contact details in stationery and other printed materials.

Sub-brand a variation on the main branding theme for a connected project making it clear that there is a link, but that the project is a separate initiative.

Sub-head the sub or cross-head is a word or phrase to attract the reader's attention. It refers to the information that follows, breaks up the text and intrigues the reader.

Tasters samples from your leaflets or other products to attract interest and orders.

Tease a device used on the front of newsletters and other print to draw the reader in by referring to the contents.

Template a sample document illustrating how and where to use headings, logos and other essential information. A prepared design that the user can work with to follow the charity's corporate identity.

Typesize the measure for printed letters and words. The standard size is 12pt. Large print is 14pt and above.

Video paper edit the process used by a production company to sort images and words into the relevant order before incurring the expense of compiling them in an edit suite.

Video signed version a copy of your video containing a British Sign Language translation.

Video signer a British Sign Language user who appears on a video translating voice over and interview into BSL.

Visuals the pieces of work produced by design agencies to illustrate their ideas or to show how they might approach a particular design job.

Web links an automatic connection on a Web page that allows a user to click onto an image or highlighted text and jump to another site of interest.

Web search engine a device that allows you to key in appropriate words or phrases and look for relevant sites and pages throughout the World Wide Web.

Web virtual pathways these are the links that allow you to click on particular buttons and words to travel to other pages and sites of interest.

Word count the number of words that will fit into a document. Writers are usually told how many words to write or the word count when commissioned to produce an article.

Written brief an outline of your ideas, timetable, budget etc., given to individuals and organisations commissioned to produce a product or service on your behalf.

About CAF
·········

CAF, Charities Aid Foundation, is a registered charity with a unique mission – to increase the substance of charity in the UK and overseas. It provides services that are both charitable and financial which help donors make the most of their giving and charities make the most of their resources.

Many of CAF's publications reflect the organisation's purpose: *Dimensions of the Voluntary Sector* offers the definitive financial overview of the sector, while the *Directory of Grant Making Trusts* provides the most comprehensive source of funding information available.

As an integral part of its activities, CAF works to raise standards of management in voluntary organisations. This includes the making of grants by its own Grants Council, sponsorship of the Charity Annual Report and Accounts Awards, seminars, training courses and the Charities Annual Conference, the largest regular gathering of key people from within the voluntary sector. In addition, Charitynet is now established as the leading Internet site on voluntary action.

For decades, CAF has led the way in developing tax-effective services to donors, and these are now used by more than 150,000 individuals and 2,000 of the UK's leading companies. Many are also using CAF's CharityCard, the world's first debit card designed exclusively for charitable giving. CAF's unique range of investment and administration services for charities includes the CafCash High Interest Cheque Account, two common investment funds for longer-term investment and a full appeals and subscription management service.

CAF's activities are not limited to the UK, however. Increasingly, CAF is looking to apply the same principles and develop similar services internationally, in its drive to increase the substance of charity across the world.

Other titles in the How To series

A series of one-stop guides on a variety of core activities, the titles appearing in the CAF 'How To' series are designed to provide both volunteers supporting smaller charities – in either an official or an unofficial capacity – and inexperienced salaried staff with practical information and guidance on good practice.

Applying to a Grant Making Trust A guide for fundraisers
Anne Villemur

ISBN 1–85934–033–4 £7.95
Published February 1997

Grant-making trusts of all sizes complain that many of the funding applications that they receive fail either to match their stated funding priorities or to provide a coherent explanation of the project or programme for which support is being sought. Consequently, they are not eligible for consideration.

In response to this situation, and drawing on the author's years of experience as editor of *The Directory of Grant Making Trusts*, this book provides step-by-step guidance in drawing up a well-rounded 'case for support' which contains all the information that trustees require when considering an application.

The Treasurer's Handbook *Ian Caulfeild Grant*

ISBN 1–85934–018–0 £7.95
Published August 1996

Recent legislation has reinforced the crucial role of the treasurer in voluntary organisations of all sizes, whilst the introduction of the SORP is intended to lead to a greater uniformity of practice throughout the sector.

As a treasurer's duties become more onerous, their personal, legal liability for the 'prudent management' of their organisation is thrown sharply into relief. Yet many volunteer treasurers do not have even a basic understanding of book-keeping activities.

In straightforward language, avoiding financial jargon, *The Treasurer's Handbook* outlines a treasurer's key tasks, proposes appropriate procedures and explains the basics of financial management.

Running a Local Fundraising Campaign *Janet Hilderley*

ISBN 1–85934–040–7 £9.95
Published October 1997

For many small charities or regional branches a successful local fundraising campaign can generate lasting results in terms of not only the money raised but also the enhanced public awareness of an organisation's existence and core activities. However, the work involved in planning and running a campaign can be considerable and there are undoubted risks if anything goes wrong.

It was once believed that it was possible to apply the same basic strategy developed for a national campaign to a local situation. Experience has proved that this approach seldom works and that greater account needs to be taken of local circumstances.

This guide provides practical information and advice on the enormous range of activities which can make up a local fundraising campaign, and helps readers to assess which options would be most appropriate for their charity.

Public Speaking and Presentations *Ian Gilchrist*
ISBN 1–85934–064–4 £7.95
Published January 1998

Effective Media Relations *Ian Gilchrist*
ISBN 1–85934–063–6 £7.95
Published March 1998

Payroll Giving *Willemina Bell in association
with Penny Clover*
ISBN 1–85934–061–X £7.95
Published May 1998

Running a Public Collection *Jennie Whiting*
ISBN 1–85934–60–1 £7.95
Published June 1998

**To order any of the above publications, please ring
Biblios Publishers' Distribution Services Ltd on 01403
710851. Or you can order online using our website:
www.charitynet.org/bookstore/**

Index
· · · · · · · · ·